# The Indians of the Northeast

BIBLIOGRAPHICAL SERIES
*The Newberry Library Center*
*for the History of the American Indian*

*General Editor*
Francis Jennings

*The Center Is Supported by Grants from*

The National Endowment for the Humanities
The Ford Foundation
The W. Clement and Jessie V. Stone Foundation
The Woods Charitable Fund, Inc.

# The Indians of the Northeast

## A Critical Bibliography

## ELISABETH TOOKER

Published for the Newberry Library

*Indiana University Press*

BLOOMINGTON AND LONDON

Manufactured in the United States of America

Library of Congress Cataloging in Publication Data
Tooker, Elisabeth.
The Indians of the Northeast.
(Bibliographical series - The Newberry Library, Center
for the History of the American Indian)
Includes index.
1. Indians of North America--Northeastern States--
Bibliography.  2. Woodland Indians--Bibliography.
I. Title.  II. Series: Bibliographical series.
Z1209.2.U52N688    [E78.E2]    016.974'004'97   78-3252
ISBN 0-253-33003-3    1 2 3 4 5 82 81 80 79 78

# CONTENTS

Note on This Bibliography      vii

Recommended Works      x

Bibliographical Essay

    Introduction      1

    History      7

    Coastal Indians      10

    Northern Iroquoians      21

    Upper Great Lakes Indians      30

Alphabetical List and Index      39

## NOTE ON THIS BIBLIOGRAPHY

The literature on the Indians of the Northeast is particularly rich and varied. Ever since the first European exploration of the Atlantic coastal region in the sixteenth century, various newcomers to the North American continent have sought out and published information on Indian culture, society, and history. In the first centuries after European discovery, these accounts were largely the work of explorers, missionaries, and colonial promoters; and not long after White settlement had fairly begun, also of historians. Although this work has continued into the present century, beginning in the nineteenth century another type of study — ethnological in character — began to assume importance. The reasons were several. The new nation established by the American Revolution found itself in what now would be called "an identity crisis." Separate from England, it sought to establish an identity and a history apart from the mother country, and it turned to Indian culture and history as one source of raw materials from which to build a sense of national uniqueness. At the same time, the United States government, forced to assume responsibility for treatment of the Indians, sought information on their customs in order to deal with Indians living both within its territories and on its borders. These interests combined with those of anthropology — which, along with other sciences, emerged as a distinct discipline in the nineteenth century — to give added impetus to the study of the ethnology of the American Indian.

The attitude of Whites toward the Indians has always been ambivalent; the Indian has been both romanticized as noble, untainted by the evils of civilization, and derided as an uncouth, savage animal. Ethnologists sought to avoid this controversy over "the noble savage," stressing the importance of culture in understanding the peoples of the world; and by the end of the nineteenth century the course of American ethnology was laid out. The customs of each Indian group — most often treated under the headings of material culture, social and political organization, and religion — were to be described in at least summary form, and anthropologists set about filling in the gaps in this map. In some cases so little of the culture in question was known that the ethnographer perforce started from scratch. But in most cases some ethnographic information was to be found in the historical documents, and these data provided both background and a starting point for the study of culture stability and change. In other instances, the best (and sometimes the only) description of the culture of the Indians of a region was to be found in the early accounts; in these cases the relevant ethnographic data were extracted and summarized in a form designed to facilitate understanding of the cultures of these Indians. The result of this effort was a series of basic ethnographies — overview descriptions of particular cultures — and a series of more specialized studies of certain aspects of these cultures.

This bibliography surveys this achievement. Generally, the most comprehensive ethnographic study or studies is mentioned first. There follows a listing of studies on more special aspects of the culture, sources to which the interested reader might turn for more detailed information than often is included in the basic ethnographies. Basic reference books are included in the Introduction, the various types of general surveys of information that, although not properly ethnological, provide necessary background information for such studies.

## RECOMMENDED WORKS

### For the Beginner

[68]    Harriot, Thomas, *A Briefe and True Report of the New Found Land of Virginia.*

[124]   Morgan, Lewis H., *League of the Ho-de-no-sau-nee or Iroquois.*

[150]   Radin, Paul, *The Winnebago Tribe.*

[164]   Ritzenthaler, Robert E., and Pat, *The Woodland Indians of the Western Great Lakes.*

[227]   Trigger, Bruce G., ed., *The Northeast.* Volume 15 of *Handbook of North American Indians.*

### For a Basic Library Collection

[27]    Denton, Daniel, *A Brief Description of New York: Formerly Called New Netherlands.*

[47]    Fenton, William N., ed., *Parker on the Iroquois.*

[54]    Gearing, Frederick O., *The Face of the Fox.*

[70]    Heckewelder, John, *An Account of the History, Manners, and Customs, of the Indian Nations who Once Inhabited Pennsylvania and the Neighouring States.*

[100]   Kinietz, W. Vernon, *The Indians of the Western Great Lakes, 1615–1760.*

[151] Radin, Paul, ed., *Crashing Thunder: The Autobiography of an American Indian.*

[175] Shimony, Annemarie Anrod, *Conservatism among the Iroquois at the Six Nations Reserve.*

[204] Speck, Frank G., *Penobscot Man.*

[209] Spindler, George, and Louise, *Dreamers without Power: The Menomini Indians.*

[217] Swanton, John R., *The Indian Tribes of North America.*

[222] Tooker, Elisabeth, *The Iroquois Ceremonial of Midwinter.*

[226] Trigger, Bruce G., *The Children of Aataentsic: A History of the Huron People to 1660.*

[244] Wallace, Anthony F. C., *The Death and Rebirth of the Seneca.*

[249] Wallis, Wilson D., and Ruth Sawtell Wallis, *The Micmac Indians of Eastern Canada.*

[261] Williams, Roger, *A Key into the Language of America.*

# BIBLIOGRAPHICAL ESSAY

## Introduction

The Indians of the Northeast — an area here defined as extending from Newfoundland to North Carolina and from the Atlantic Coast to the Upper Great Lakes — were not, as the English term "Indian" implies, one people. Rather, the region was occupied by a number of different peoples, each having its own distinctive language, customs, and history and pursuing a different course of action in the years following the European discovery of the continent.

Nonetheless, the seventeenth-century Europeans dealing with the Northeastern Indians quickly learned that most of the languages of the region resembled either that spoken by the Algonkin Indians living in the Saint Lawrence valley or those spoken by the Iroquois Indians in what is now upstate New York. This has remained the basic classification. Except for a few Siouan speakers, all the Indians of the Northeast spoke languages belonging to what are now called the Algonquian and the Iroquoian language families.

This linguistic classification is also a cultural classification. As the seventeenth-century French missionaries discovered and the ethnologists later confirmed, the cultures of the various Iroquoian-speaking Indians resembled each other both in basic plan and in a number of particulars. Further, the cultures of the various Algonquian-speaking peoples — although in many respects different from those of the Iroquoians — also resembled each other in some detail. Consequently, the terms Iroquoian and Algonquian have come to be used to refer not only to the two principal language families in the region but to the major cultural divisions as well.

The Northeast is conveniently subdivided into three ethnological regions: Coastal, Lower Great Lakes, and Upper Great Lakes. The Coastal region, roughly corresponding to the area of White settlement in the seventeenth and eighteenth centuries, was inhabited by speakers of various Algonquian languages and, in the extreme southern part, some Iroquoian- and Siouan-speakers. The region around the Lower Great Lakes was occupied by speakers of various Northern Iroquoian languages, including the Iroquois proper. The Upper Great Lakes region (here defined as including the Ohio valley) was inhabited by speakers of various Algonquian languages and one Siouan-speaking group, the Winnebagos.

For names and locations of the various Indian groups in these three regions of the Northeast a still-useful reference is *The Handbook of American Indians North of Mexico*, edited by Frederick Webb Hodge [79] and published by the Bureau of American Ethnology in two volumes in 1907 and 1910. Arranged alphabetically, its entries include sketches of the history and culture of various Indian tribes, brief biographies of famous Indians, and descriptions of some special aspects of North American Indian cultures. Also included at the end of each tribal sketch is a synonymy of tribal names found in the historical documents. The *Handbook* grew out of a project to collect such names that for many years engaged the staff of the Bureau of American Ethnology, now defunct but at that time a leading center of anthropological research. As variant spellings were collected, these lists of synonymies became particularly extensive. Some of the same information published in the *Handbook* may be found in John Swanton's *The Indian Tribes of North America* [217]. Organized according to present state boundaries, this work lists the tribes that inhabited each state, their principal names, linguistic affiliations, subdivisions and villages, major events in their history, and population estimates. Also included are maps of the area.

A more up-to-date review of these basic data is found in the Northeast volume of the *Handbook of North American Indians* [227], to be published by the Smithsonian Institution. Designed to provide more extensive coverage than the old *Handbook* edited by Hodge, this new handbook contains articles on the culture and history of each tribe as well as more general survey articles on Indian culture and history. The encyclopedic nature of this work makes it useful for both those who seek an introduction to the anthropological studies of North American Indians and those seeking a review of current knowledge on the subject.

Locations and linguistic affiliations of the Northeastern tribes are also given in George Peter Murdock and Timothy J. O'Leary, *Ethnographic Bibliography of North America* [126], an indispensable research tool for the student of North American Indians. The bibliographical entries (which include articles as well as books and monographs) are arranged by tribe and region. Also included are sections on materials less specifically divided by tribe and region. The latest (fourth) edition of this bibliography lists items published through 1972. The two volumes of the *Anthropological Bibliography of the Eastern Seaboard* [165, 61] cover much the same ethnographic materials on the Coastal Indians as the Murdock and O'Leary *Ethnographic Bibliography* but are valuable for the more extensive listing of archeological and historical writings. An even more detailed listing of these items relating to the Northern Iroquoians, with some annotation, is Paul L. Weinman's *A Bibliography of the Iroquoian Literature* [255]. James Constantine Pilling's bibliographies of writings on and about the Algonquian languages [142] and Iroquoian languages [141] are still the most useful guides to the early publications in these languages, including such items as prayer books, hymnals, catechisms, school primers, spelling books, and readers as well as dictionaries and grammars. William N. Fenton's bibliographical essay "Indian and White Relations in Eastern North America," in *American Indian and White Relations to 1830* [46] is a knowledgeable survey of writings on the eastern Indians. This volume also contains a lengthy, although selective, bibliography with some annotation including reference volumes, manuscripts, and ethnological and historical works.

In addition to the *Handbook of North American Indians*, summary descriptions of Northeastern Indian cultures are found in various books on North American Indians written for the general reader. A very readable and still useful book of this sort is Clark Wissler's *Indians of the United States* [267], first published in 1940. Ruth Underhill's *Red Man's America* [231], a textbook on North American Indians, and her *Red Man's Religion* [232], a companion volume, also contain summaries of Indian cultures of the region. Another text surveying North American Indian cultures is Harold Driver's *Indians of North America* [31], which includes maps of the distribution of particular culture traits as well as summary descriptions. However, scholars as well as others desiring detailed information on the distribution of particular culture traits will find Driver and Massey's earlier *Comparative Studies of North American Indians* [32] more useful. A collection of papers surveying Northeastern Indian cultures and history, including one by A. I. Hallowell on psychological characteristics and one by Margaret W. Fisher on mythology, have been published in *Man in Northeastern North America*, edited by Frederick Johnson [93].

The various recent classifications of North American languages, such as the Voegelin and Voegelin map [236], derive with some modification from Edward Sapir's [168] famous 1929 classification. In part, Sapir's classification rests on the earlier Powell map, based on work done at the Bureau of American Ethnology [144], which in its turn is a revision of Albert Gallatin's earlier study in his *Synopsis* [53], a work that is also of interest for its survey of scholarly knowledge of Indians at the time it was published (1836). Current knowledge regarding the classification of the Indian languages of the Northeast is summarized in two articles in *Native Languages of the Americas*, edited by Thomas A. Sebeok [170]: "Algonquian," by Karl V. Teeter, and "Siouan, Iroquoian, and Caddoan," by Wallace L. Chafe.

A summary of the archeology of the Northeast is contained in Gordon R. Willey's masterly survey, *An Introduction to American Archaeology* [259]. A less technical survey, and one that perhaps serves better as a first introduction to the subject, is Dean Snow, *The Archaeology of North America* [192]. Summaries of various aspects of Northeastern archeology are found in the articles of *Archeology of Eastern United States*, edited by James B. Griffin [60]. The archeology of the western part of this region is surveyed in George Irving Quimby's *Indian Life in the Upper Great Lakes, 11,000 B.C. to A.D. 1800* [146], a book that also includes ethnographic sketches of the historical tribes in the area. In *Indian Culture and European Trade Goods* [147], Quimby supplements his earlier work, providing a discussion of the archeology of the region in the historic period. In addition, two state archeological histories merit special mention: William A. Ritchie's *The Archaeology of New York State* [160] and James E. Fitting's *The Archaeology of Michigan* [49].

Of all the archeological remains in the region, the earthworks found especially in the Ohio and Mississippi valleys have excited the most interest. Discovered when settlers moved into this region after the American Revolution, they provided material for much speculation on the identity of their builders; Egyptians, Hebrews, Tartars, Phoenicians, Picts, and Hindus were among those suggested. Only after a century of controversy was the matter put to rest. The history of this controversy is contained in Robert Silverberg's *Mound Builders of Ancient America* [177]. A number of these earthworks were destroyed, and for these, as well as for those that still remain, the best published plans are often those in Squier and Davis, *Ancient Monuments of the Mississippi Valley* [212]. Squier's *Aboriginal Monuments of the State of New York* [211] is a kind of companion volume extending his earlier work into New York State. Important twentieth-century surveys of these archeological cultures include Henry Clyde Shetrone, *The Mound-Builders* [174], William S. Webb and Charles E. Snow, *The Adena People* [254], William S. Webb and Raymond S. Baby, *The Adena People No. 2* [253], and Don W. Dragoo, *Mounds for the Dead* [30].

## History

After the discovery of the New World by Europeans, the lives of Indians and Whites on the North American continent became increasingly intertwined, as did their histories. The earliest exploration of the region by Whites may well have had a greater impact on European societies than on Indians — the brief appearance of a few Europeans in Indian country affected Indian life less than the accounts of explorers aroused curiosity and speculation, as well as affecting economic interests in Europe. Be that as it may, Indian life did not remain unaffected by this contact. In the sixteenth century — a century that witnessed no permanent White settlements in the area — European-introduced diseases began taking their toll, and trade for European-produced goods began to alter inter-tribal relations as well as Indian cultures themselves. In the seventeenth century, as Whites established permanent settlements in the region, the contest began between France and England for control of the continent, a contest motivated primarily by desire to control the fur trade. A readable and still useful account of the seventeenth- and eighteenth-century conflict is Francis Parkman's multivolume classic *France and England in North America* [134]. Although Parkman has been much criticized for his Boston Brahmin bias, his work has much to commend it. For example, Parkman discusses the differing and sometimes conflicting policies of various Indian tribes in this period, a matter often ignored by twentieth-century historians, who are apt to lump all tribes together and treat them simply as "Indians." Nevertheless, more recent histories of this period contain valuable data and perspective. These include Douglas Leach's *The Northern Colonial Frontier, 1607–1763* [107] and W. J. Eccles's two volumes, *The Canadian Frontier, 1534–1760* [36] and *France in America* [37]. Eccles also has discussed the history of the latter half of the seventeenth century in two other books, *Frontenac: The Courtier Governor* [34] and *Canada under Louis XIV* [35]. Although first published in 1853, the *History of the*

*Catholic Missions among the Indian Tribes of the United States*, by the noted Catholic historian John Gilmary Shea [172], remains the most comprehensive account of Catholic missionary work and of the missionaries themselves, some of whom wrote invaluable accounts of the Indians.

The history of the northeastern portion of the Northeast as it more specifically relates to the Indians up to 1660 is discussed by Bruce G. Trigger in his comprehensive history of the Hurons, *The Children of Aataentsic* [226]. Intertribal trade and wars in the seventeenth century are also described in George T. Hunt, *The Wars of the Iroquois* [85]. This book is, however, an overwritten account that needs some corrective such as that suggested by Allen W. Trelease in his article "The Iroquois and the Western Fur Trade" [224]. Thomas Elliot Norton, in *The Fur Trade in Colonial New York, 1686–1776* [128], takes up the subject from the end of the period considered in Hunt's *Wars of the Iroquois* to the time of the American Revolution. A more detailed discussion of the relationship between Whites and Indians living in what is now New York State in the seventeenth century is to be found in Allen W. Trelease, *Indian Affairs in Colonial New York* [223].

In the nineteenth century, the study of the cultures and history of Indians was taken up by the newly emerging field of anthropology. In fact, until World War II the history of American anthropology was virtually a history of anthropological study of the Indians. A. Irving Hallowell has surveyed this nineteenth-century work, its aims and accomplishments, in his excellent long paper, "The Beginnings of Anthropology in America" [64]. The development of linguistic studies of American Indian languages in the nineteenth and twentieth centuries has been reviewed in another excellent study by Floyd Lounsbury, "One Hundred Years of Anthropological Linguistics" [113], and more briefly in an article by Harry Hoijer in *Native Languages of the Americas*, edited by Thomas A. Sebeok [170]. The best survey of the development of archeological research is *A History of American Archaeology*, by Gordon R. Willey and Jeremy A. Sabloff [260]. The history of archeological work in the Northeast is summarized in David S. Brose's paper "The Northeastern United States," in the volume of regional histories of archeological work edited by James E. Fitting *The Development of North American Archaeology* [16].

## Coastal Indians

The Indians along the eastern seaboard from Newfoundland to North Carolina lived in small local groups. Although these groups had names, a number of which appear in local histories, ethnologists often have found it convenient to classify under a single name those with very similar cultures. This classification is used here. For some of the local groups there is so little ethnographic information that no standard work can be cited. Consequently the reader may well find no reference given for a particular group, and in these cases he should consult the standard reference books cited above.

For those Indian groups of this region on which there is ethnographic information, the best descriptions are often early ones. Because they occupied regions that were settled early by colonists and decimated by White-introduced diseases and by wars with both Whites and Indians, only remnants of their population and cultures have survived into this century. Thus, not only are the descriptions written in earlier centuries often the best, sometimes they are the only such descriptions.

The material in these early descriptions, as well as in more recent works on the Algonquians of this region, has been used by Regina Flannery in her *Analysis of Coastal Algonquian Culture* [50]. This study, which despite its title also includes material on the Northern Iroquoian-speaking Hurons and Iroquois, is a comparison of culture traits. Hence, although not easy to read, it affords a useful overview of the cultures of the region.

One of the groups whose culture is known only through the historical documents is the Beothuk people of Newfoundland, a group in early contact with Whites because of the importance of European fishing in the region beginning in the sixteenth century. This material, though not as extensive as one would wish, has been assembled by James P. Howley in *The Beothucks or Red Indians* [81], the most comprehensive book on these Indians.

More information is to be found on the Algonquian-speaking Indians of the Gaspé, the Maritime

Provinces, and Maine, peoples sometimes collectively termed the Abnakis, although this term also has been used to refer only to the more southerly of these groups and to the confederacy composed of the Penobscots, Passamaquoddies, Malecites, and Micmacs. The history of this confederacy has been discussed by Frank G. Speck in "The Eastern Algonquian Wabanaki Confederacy" [194]. A number of tales from these groups are given in Charles G. Leland's *The Algonquin Legends of New England* [109].

For the most northerly of these peoples, the Micmacs, the most important early sources are Nicolas Denys's *The Description and Natural History of the Coasts of North America* [28] and Chrestien Le Clercq's *New Relation of Gaspesia* [108]. An extensive description of various aspects of Micmac culture, based on fieldwork done early in this century and on the historical accounts, is contained in Wilson D. and Ruth Sawtell Wallis, *The Micmac Indians of Eastern Canada* [249]. Philip K. Bock has described more recent life on one reserve in *The Micmac Indians of Restigouche* [11], which, like many other recent ethnographies of Indians of this northern region, contains material from the historical documents. The history of the Micmacs is also surveyed in Wilson D. Wallis, "Historical Background of the Micmac Indians of Canada" [251]. Culture change in the first half of this century is treated by the Wallises in "Culture Loss and Culture Change among the Micmac of the Canadian Maritime Provinces, 1912–1950" [248]. A number of Micmac tales are collected in Silas

T. Rand, *Legends of the Micmacs* [159], and in Elsie Clews Parsons, "Micmac Folklore" [135], as well as in the Wallises' *Micmac Indians*. Some religious beliefs are given by Frederick Johnson in his "Notes on Micmac Shamanism" [92].

The data on the Malecites are less full. Studies of their culture include W. H. Mechling, *The Malecite Indians* [118], Wilson D. and Ruth Sawtell Wallis, *The Malecite Indians of New Brunswick* [250], and Nicholas N. Smith, *Notes on the Malecite of Woodstock, New Brunswick* [191]. Mechling also collected a number of myths and tales that are published in his *Malecite Tales* [117].

The material and social life of the Penobscots is described in Frank G. Speck, *Penobscot Man* [204], and their religion is discussed in his *Penobscot Shamanism* [196]. A few other religious practices and a number of tales are given in his "Penobscot Tales and Religious Beliefs" [202]. Some myths of the Wawenocks, a group living west of the Penobscots, and some history of this group are given in Frank G. Speck, "Wawenock Myth Texts from Maine" [200].

The Indians of southern New England were more greatly affected by early White contact than were those of northern New England, and consequently our knowledge of the culture of these Indians is even more dependent on the seventeenth-century accounts. The best of these accounts, and one of the most interesting of all books on North American Indians, is Roger Williams's *Key into the Language of America* [261]. The title is somewhat misleading. It is essentially a phrase book with observations on the customs of the Narragansetts — a reminder that Whites at the time were foreigners in a land largely governed by Indians and needed the same kinds of aid as present-day travelers and new residents need in foreign lands. Perhaps the two most important descriptions of Massachusetts Indians — contemporary with Roger Williams's description of the Indians of Rhode Island but written in a more conventional style — are found in William Wood, *New England's Prospect* [268], and Thomas Morton, *New English Canaan* [125].

The material in these and other accounts of the cultures of New England Indians is surveyed in Charles C. Willoughby, *Antiquities of the New England Indians* [266], a book that also discusses the archeology of the region. Willoughby gives a somewhat more extensive description of the available data on some of the subjects mentioned in this book in two articles: "Dress and Ornaments of the New England Indians" [263] and "Houses and Gardens of the New England Indians" [264]. A somewhat comparable survey, but one that includes a more detailed discussion of the data on social organization and religion than does Willoughby's, is Froelich G. Rainey, "Compilation of Historical Data Contributing to the Ethnography of Connecticut and Southern New England Indians" [158]. Additional ethnographic information on the Mohegan Indians is found in Frank G. Speck, "Notes on the Mohegan and Niantic Indians" [193].

The most comprehensive seventeenth-century accounts of the changes in the life of New England Indians are by Daniel Gookin [56, 57], a colleague of John Eliot, the noted missionary who translated the Bible into Algonquian. An account of a twentieth-century New England Indian group is given by George L. Hicks and David I. Kertzer in "Making a Middle Way" [78], and Ethel Boissevain has described contemporary Narragansett life in "The Detribalization of the Narragansett Indians" [12] and "Narragansett Survival" [13]. The history of the Mahicans is summarized in Ted J. Brasser, *Riding on the Frontier's Crest* [14], and that of the Stockbridge group is covered in Marion Johnson Mochon, "Stockbridge-Munsee Cultural Adaptations" [120].

New Englanders, ever conscious of what they saw as their role in history, wrote a number of accounts of the wars between themselves and the Indians, accounts that have provided material for a number of histories. A modern history of King Philip's War, based on these sources, is Douglas E. Leach, *Flintlock and Tomahawk* [106]. Puritan-Indian relationships including missionary influence until the outbreak of King Philip's War in 1675 are detailed in Alden T. Vaughan's most useful study, *New England Frontier* [233]. The nature of these relationships is also the subject of Francis Jennings's history of this region during the same period, *The Invasion of America: Indians, Colonialism, and the Cant of Conquest* [88]. New England history as it pertains more specifically to Connecticut is given in John W. De Forest's *History of the Indians of Connecticut from the Earliest Known Period to 1850* [25].

The ethnographic data on the Indians of eastern New York State are no more extensive than those on other Coastal Algonquians. By far the most comprehensive seventeenth-century account of the Indians who lived in the New York City area is contained in Daniel Denton, *Brief Description of New York* [27], although, as the title indicates, the description is brief. E. M. Ruttenber's *History of the Indian Tribes of Hudson's River* [166] is a century-old history of the region. A more detailed and scholarly history of the Algonquian Indians of New York is in Allen W. Trelease, *Indian Affairs in Colonial New York* [223].

Although unfortunately short, one of the best early descriptions of the Indians of the Delaware valley is contained in a letter written by William Penn in 1683 to the Committee of the Free Society of Traders [139]. Delaware Indian culture is also described in an earlier Swedish account of the region, Peter Lindeström's *Geographia Americae* [110].

Later accounts of the Indians of Pennsylvania include John Heckewelder's important *Account of the History, Manners, and Customs, of the Indian Natives who Once Inhabited Pennsylvania and the Neighbouring States* [70] and David Zeisberger's *History* [83]. Both Heckewelder and Zeisberger were Moravian missionaries, and the early history of Moravian work is given in George Henry Loskiel's *History of the Mission of the United Breth-*

*ren in North America* [112]. A recent popular survey of Pennsylvania Indians is Paul A. W. Wallace's *Indians in Pennsylvania* [247]. The history of the western part of the state and adjacent regions to 1795 is given more extended treatment in Randolph C. Downes, *Council Fires on the Upper Ohio* [29].

In this century, some effort has been devoted to learning more about traditional Delaware (also called Lenape) culture from Delawares now living in Oklahoma and in Ontario. This work has resulted in the publication of M. R. Harrington's "Preliminary Sketch of Lenape Culture" [66] and his more extended description of Delaware religion, particularly the Big House ceremony, *Religion and Ceremonies of the Lenape* [67]. The latter subject was also studied by Frank G. Speck, who published the results of his investigation in *A Study of the Delaware Indian Big House Ceremony* [201]. Some other Delaware rites are described in Speck's *Oklahoma Delaware Ceremonies, Feasts and Dances* [203]. Delaware belief and practice, particularly as it related to curing, is discussed by Gladys Tantaquidgeon in her *Study of Delaware Indian Medicine Practice and Folk Beliefs* [218]. The modern peyote cult among the Delawares is the subject of Vincenzo Petrullo's *The Diabolic Root* [140].

William W. Newcomb has summarized the data relative to Delaware culture in the various ethnographic accounts and historical documents in *The Culture and Acculturation of the Delaware Indians* [127]. His discussion is detailed enough to provide a most useful overview of what is known about Delaware Indian culture. C. A. Weslager has described the complex history of this people in *The Delaware Indians* [258], and Anthony F. C. Wallace gives much eighteenth-century Delaware history in the biography, *King of the Delawares: Teedyuscung, 1700–1763* [242].

The Walam Olum manuscript, purported to be the Delawares' own traditional account of their history, is reproduced in Daniel G. Brinton, *The Lenape and Their Legends* [15], a book that also provides some survey of Delaware culture, language, and history. The authenticity of the Walam Olum manuscript has frequently been questioned, although Voegelin and others have argued for its credibility in *Walam Olum, or Red Score* [241].

There is less published information on the Nanticokes. Some description of Nanticoke culture, as it survived into the early decades of this century, is given in Frank G. Speck, *The Nanticoke Community of Delaware* [195]. The history of the Nanticokes, especially as it relates to Pennsylvania, is given in C. A. Weslager, *The Nanticoke Indians: A Refugee Tribal Group of Pennsylvania* [257]. A description of the life of these Indians in recent times and some account of their history is also given in C. A. Weslager, *Delaware's Forgotten Folk* [256]. Some additional ethnographic and historical data, much from the Nanticokes living in Canada, are found in Speck's *The Nanticoke and Conoy Indians* [198].

Some of the best information on the Southeastern Algonquians, as the various Algonquian-speaking groups of Virginia and North Carolina have been termed, and virtually all that is known about the North Carolina Algonquians, is contained in accounts of the Ralegh expeditions in the latter part of the sixteenth century. These records include the famous watercolors of John White, which have recently been reproduced in an authoritative edition with valuable commentary, *The American Drawings of John White*, by Paul Hulton and David Beers Quinn [84]. More accessible to most readers are the reproductions of these paintings in Stefan Lorant's *The New World* [111]. White's drawings were used by De Bry for his almost equally famous engravings, first published in 1590 with accompanying description of the country and the Indians who lived there in Thomas Harriot's *A Briefe and True Report of the New Found Land of Virginia* [68]. Various other records of these early expeditions are found in Quinn's *The Roanoke Voyages, 1584–1590* [148].

The ethnographic information contained in the sixteenth- and seventeenth-century sources is summarized in Charles C. Willoughby, "Virginia Indians in the Seventeenth Century" [265]. The twentieth-century remnants of these Indians and their culture are described in Frank G. Speck, *Chapters on the Ethnology of the Powhatan Tribes of Virginia* [199]. The history of the Powhatan Confederacy (a confederation that included some but not all of these tribes) from the sixteenth to the twentieth century is found in James Mooney, "The Powhatan Confederacy, Past and Present" [122]. The history of the Chickahominies, a somewhat alien enclave within the Powhatan tribes, is in Theodore Stern, *Chickahominy: The Changing Culture of a Virginia Indian Community* [213]. An account of the Rappahannock Indians, with special attention to survival of elements of older Indian cultures, is given in Frank G. Speck, *The Rappahannock Indians of Virginia* [197].

Two other language families besides Algonquian are represented in the southern part of the Coastal region: Siouan and Iroquoian. The location, history, and culture of the various Siouan-speaking Indians in this area is surveyed in James Mooney, *The Siouan Tribes of the East* [121]. The history of the best-known of these peoples is given in Charles M. Hudson's *The Catawba Nation* [82]. Given the paucity of ethnographic information on these Siouan groups, Frank G. Speck's description of a Tutelo ceremony as it was performed in Canada, *The Tutelo Spirit Adoption Ceremony* [205], is of more than ordinary interest.

Of the Iroquoian peoples of this area, the Tuscaroras are the best known; in part because a number joined the League of the Iroquois in the eighteenth century, becoming known as the sixth nation of that confederacy (see end of section on "Northern Iroquoians" below). The history of two lesser-known Iroquoian groups of the Virginia–North Carolina area, the Nottaways and Meherrins is surveyed in Lewis R. Binford, "An Ethnohistory of the Nottaway, Meherrin and Weanock Indians of Southeastern Virginia" [7].

## Northern Iroquoians

Although the lives of Indians living in the Atlantic Coast region were greatly affected by the presence of Whites who settled in these lands, the lives of those in the more interior Great Lakes area were not so influenced until the latter years of the eighteenth century. Rather, up until the American Revolution, the influence of Western civilization in this region was of quite a different sort, one that was intimately bound up with the fur trade instead of colonization. Nonetheless, this period witnessed considerable change in Indian ways of life. It included not only an increasing dependence on European trade goods, but also the migration of some tribes and the extinction of others. Of all the Iroquoian-speaking peoples of the Lower Great Lakes area, the five tribes of the Iroquois Confederacy gained the most from the fur trade. Located in a particularly advantageous geographic area, they successfully utilized it to rise to a position of power in the Northeast and were largely responsible for the dissolution or emigration of other Iroquoian peoples of the region, leaving only remnants of these Iroquoian-speakers. The location and villages of the various Iroquian peoples, along with some brief history, is given in William N. Fenton, "Problems Arising from the Historic Northeastern Position of the Iroquois" [41].

In the sixteenth century, Jacques Cartier found Iroquoian-speakers living in the Saint Lawrence valley, but they had abandoned the region by the time of Samuel de Champlain's exploration of the river, and Champlain found only Algonquian-speakers residing there. Most of what is known of these Laurentian Iroquoians is found in the descriptions of Cartier's second and third voyages [6]. These data as they relate to the Laurentian Iroquoians at Hochelaga are discussed in some detail in James F. Pendergast and Bruce G. Trigger, *Cartier's Hochelaga and the Dawson Site* [138].

More is known about the Iroquoian-speaking Hurons, who, until they were defeated by the Iroquois in 1649, were an important trading ally of the French. Most of this information on Huron culture is found in three sources: the great *Jesuit Relations* [220], the yearly accounts of the Jesuit missionaries on their work in New France; the account of Champlain's visit in 1615–1616 [5]; and Gabriel Sagard's description, *The Long Journey to the Country of the Hurons* [167], which is based in part on Champlain's work. The data in these documents as they relate to Huron culture have been compiled by Elisabeth Tooker in her *Ethnography of the Huron Indians, 1615–1649* [221]. These data are also summarized in Bruce G. Trigger's more popular description, *The Huron: Farmers of the North* [225], and have been used by Conrad Heidenreich in his study of the economy of the Hurons, *Huronia: A History and Geography of the Huron Indians, 1600–1650* [71], a book that also includes a useful discussion of the location of Huron villages. The history of the Hurons is given in Trigger's long and definitive study, *The Children of Aataentsic* [226], a work that is a model of how ethnohistory ought to be written as well as one essential to the understanding of the history of the Northeast.

After their defeat, a group of Hurons and Petuns moved west, and in the eighteenth century they became known to the English as Wyandots. The social organization of this Iroquoian group in the nineteenth century is summarized in John Wesley Powell's "Wyandot Government" [143], and their traditions are given in two publications by Marius Barbeau, *Huron and Wyandot Mythology* [2] and *Huron-Wyandot Traditional Narratives* [3]. Peter Dooyentate Clarke's *Origin and Traditional History of the Wyandots* [20] is of some interest, since Clarke was himself a Wyandot.

Although probably more is known of the seventeenth-century culture of the Hurons than of any other Indian people living in the Northeast at the time, there are very few data on the other Northern Iroquoians defeated by the Iroquois Five Nations in the middle of the seventeenth century: the Petuns, Neutrals, Eries, and Susquehannocks. Such data as exist on the Neutral Indians have been brought together by Gordon Wright in his *The Neutral Indians: A Source Book* [269]. The history of the defeat of the Susquehannocks is given in Francis Jennings, "Glory, Death, and Transfiguration: The Susquehannock Indians in the Seventeenth Century" [87].

Although the ethnographic literature on the Iroquois is the most extensive of that on any North American Indian group save the Navajos, the best single description, despite its nineteenth-century style, is Lewis H. Morgan's classic *League of the Ho-de-no-sau-nee or Iroquois* [124], first published in 1851. It has been republished several times, including an edition first published in 1901 that contains useful notes by Herbert M. Lloyd. A shorter and more recent description of Iroquois culture has been provided by Frank G. Speck in a pamphlet titled *The Iroquois* [206]. Hazel Hertzberg, *The Great Tree and the Longhouse* [74], is another useful, if brief, description of Iroquois culture. Written for seventh-graders, it incorporates some important recent anthropological work on the Iroquois. Another short survey description is Buell Quain, "The Iroquois" [145]. A longer description based on the historical and ethnographic accounts, although marred by some misinterpretation of these accounts, is Sara Henry Stites, *Economics of the Iroquois* [214]. A briefer, similar description of the Mohawks, one that focuses on culture change rather than economics, is Mary Rowell Carse, *The Mohawk Iroquois* [18]. A more extended popular book on Iroquois culture and history is Thomas R. Henry, *Wilderness Messiah* [73], a work also marred by some misconstruing of the data. In contrast, Annemarie Shimony's lengthy description of traditional Iroquois culture, *Conservatism among the Iroquois at the Six Nations Reserve* [175], is based on fieldwork on the large Six Nations Reserve in Canada. It contains much valuable detail on Iroquois culture, including political and social organization and religion, and is, next to Morgan's *League*, the most important general ethnographic description of the Iroquois.

Although no study of Iroquois culture and society has equalled Morgan's *League of the Iroquois*, the ethnographic studies that have appeared since its publication provide more detailed descriptions of topics briefly described by Morgan. The traditions of the Iroquois Confederacy (the League of the Iroquois), including those important ones incorporated into the Condolence Council, the ceremony at which new chiefs are installed, are the subject of Horatio Hale's important *The Iroquois Book of Rites* [63], William M. Beauchamp's *Civil, Religious and Mourning Councils and Ceremonies of Adoption* [4], and Duncan Scott's "Traditional History of the Confederacy of the Six Nations" [169]. The last, an account prepared by the chiefs at the Six Nations Reserve and approved in 1900, is also published in Arthur C. Parker's *Constitution of the Five Nations* [132] along with an earlier version by Seth Newhouse. The history of these versions is discussed by William N. Fenton in his introduction to *Parker on the Iroquois* [47], a book that reprints Parker's three major monographs, one of which is the *Constitution of the Five Nations.* Fenton has also written the most comprehensive and best introduction to the matter of names of the chiefs of the League in his *The Roll Call of the Iroquois Chiefs* [44] and has edited "The Requickening Address of the Iroquois Condolence Council," by J. N. B. Hewitt [77]. Both the Roll Call and the Requickening Address are important rituals of the Condolence Council. Paul A. W. Wallace has provided a popular compilation of the traditions of the League in *The White Roots of Peace* [246].

In addition to the descriptions in Morgan's and Shimony's studies, information on the major calendric ceremonies of the Iroquois religion is found in Fenton's *Outline of Seneca Ceremonies at Coldspring Longhouse* [38] and "Tonawanda Longhouse Ceremonies: Ninety Years after Lewis Henry Morgan" [42] and in Frank G. Speck's *Midwinter Rites of the Cayuga Long House* [207]. These and other nineteenth- and twentieth-century accounts are discussed in Elisabeth Tooker, *The Iroquois Ceremonial of Midwinter* [222]. The songs and dances that form an integral part of Iroquois ceremonies have been more fully described in Gertrude Kurath, *Iroquois Music and Dance* [101] and *Dance and Song Rituals of the Six Nations Reserve* [102]. The Thanksgiving Speech, another important rite in these ceremonies, is given both in text and in translation in Wallace L. Chafe, *Seneca Thanksgiving Rituals* [19]. This speech, even in translation, conveys something of the famous Iroquois oratorial ability as well as insight into the nature of Iroquois cosmology. This Thanksgiving Address is also the subject of Michael K. Foster, *From the Earth to beyond the Sky* [52], which, like Chafe's study, contains some excellent discussion of the speech itself.

Although Iroquois False Face masks are familiar to many from museum exhibits and the like, the literature on them is not as extensive as might be supposed. The most important descriptions include Fenton's two articles, "The Seneca Society of Faces" [39] and "Masked Medicine Societies of the Iroquois" [40]; Joseph Keppler, "Comments on Certain Iroquois

Masks" [98]; Alanson Skinner, "Some Seneca Masks and Their Use" [184]; Robert Ritzenthaler, *Iroquois False-face Masks* [163]; Jean Hendry, *Iroquois Masks and Maskmaking at Onondaga* [72]; and Harold Blau, "Function and the False Faces" [10]. The rituals and legends of the Eagle Society are given extensive description in Fenton's *The Iroquois Eagle Dance* [45]. Both the False Face and the Eagle Society, as well as the other medicine societies, are discussed by Arthur C. Parker in "Secret Medicine Societies of the Seneca" [129] and by Shimony [175] and Speck [207].

Several long versions of the Iroquois origin myth, collected by J. N. B. Hewitt, are published in the two parts of his *Iroquoian Cosmology* [75, 76]. Other Iroquois myths and legends are found in Harriet Maxwell Converse, *Myths and Legends of the New York State Iroquois* [21]; Jeremiah Curtin and J. N. B. Hewitt, *Seneca Fiction, Legends, and Myths* [23]; Jesse J. Cornplanter, *Legends of the Longhouse* [22]; Arthur C. Parker, *Seneca Myths and Folk Tales* [133]; and Erminnie A. Smith, *Myths of the Iroquois* [187].

Beginning in 1799 when he had his first vision, and ending in 1815 with his death, the Seneca chief Handsome Lake had a series of visions in which messengers from the Creator told him what the Creator wanted the Iroquois to do. After Handsome Lake's death, these messages, along with some account of Handsome Lake's life, came to be recalled annually in a long speech known as the Code of Handsome Lake. The longest published version of this speech is contained in Arthur C. Parker, *The Code of Handsome Lake, the Seneca Prophet* [131]. The social and political circumstances of the Iroquois during Handsome Lake's lifetime and an extended account of his life are given by Anthony F. C. Wallace in *The Death and Rebirth of the Seneca* [244].

Two other men, both contemporaries of Handsome Lake, were particularly prominent in Iroquois affairs at the time and merited biographies by William L. Stone. One was the noted Seneca orator Red Jacket, a number of whose elegant speeches are to be found in Stone's *The Life and Times of Red Jacket, or Sa-go-ye-wat-ha* [216]. The other was Joseph Brant, the Mohawk leader of the pro-British Iroquois forces in the American Revolution and later leader of those Iroquois who chose to settle along the Grand River on the Six Nations Reserve in Canada. His career is discussed in Stone's two-volume *Life of Joseph Brant – Thayendanegea* [215]. Although this biography contains material on Iroquois participation in the Revolution, that history is treated more fully in Barbara Graymont's *The Iroquois in the American Revolution* [58].

The most extensive description of Iroquois foods and their preparation is one written by F. W. Waugh, *Iroquois Foods and Food Preparation* [252]. Another long discussion is that by Arthur C. Parker in *Iroquois Uses of Maize and Other Food Plants* [130]. M. R. Harrington also wrote an article on the subject, "Some Seneca Corn-foods and Their Preparation" [65]. Some discussion of medicinal plants used by the Iroquois is given in William N. Fenton, "Contacts between Iroquois Herbalism and Colonial Medicine" [43].

The material culture of the Iroquois is described in various publications mentioned above, notably in Morgan's *League of the Iroquois* [124], which incorporates descriptions of artifacts Morgan collected for the New York State Museum, and Speck's *The Iroquois* [206]. It is also the subject of Carrie Lyford's *Iroquois Crafts* [116], a pamphlet that provides a useful survey of this aspect of Iroquois culture. The best recent description of wampum is contained in Fenton's discussion of the wampum belts in the New York State Museum, "The New York State Wampum Collection: The Case for the Integrity of Cultural Treasures" [48].

A brief account of the history and culture of the Tuscarora Indians, who began moving to what is now New York State and who joined the league as the sixth nation in the early decades of the eighteenth century, is contained in Anthony F. C. Wallace, *The Modal Personality Structure of the Tuscarora* [243]. The history of the Tuscaroras is most fully given in F. Roy Johnson, *The Tuscaroras* [91], a work that incorporates data from Elias Johnson's earlier *History of the Tuscarora Indians* [90]. Two recently published books — an autobiography of Clinton Rickard [59] and a collection of reminiscences by Ted C. Williams [262] — provide some account of recent reservation life from personal points of view.

## Upper Great Lakes Indians

Like the Iroquois, the Indians of the Upper Great Lakes region were much affected, both directly and indirectly, by the fur trade in the seventeenth and eighteenth centuries and by White settlement in the nineteenth century. Consequently, the historical documents provide most of the available information for some groups and contain valuable data for all of them. W. Vernon Kinietz, in *The Indians of the Western Great Lakes, 1615–1760* [100], includes a survey of these data for the Miamis and Potawatomis as well as the Hurons.

The cultures of the Indians of this region as a whole are described by Robert E. and Pat Ritzenthaler using the standard ethnographic categories — food quest, life cycle, social organization, material culture, religion, games, and folklore — in *The Woodland Indians of the Western Great Lakes* [164]. Written for the general reader, it provides an introduction to the subject for those having little or no knowledge of Indians and gives a convenient overview to more knowledgeable persons. An extensive and technical comparison of what is known of the kinship systems of most of the Indians of this region has been provided by Charles Callender in his *Social Organization of the Central Algonkian Indians* [17]. A comparison of burial customs of groups in this area is in Erminie Wheeler Voegelin, *Mortuary Customs of the Shawnee and Other Eastern Tribes* [240]. Richard Asa Yarnell has provided a detailed survey of the wild and cultivated plants used by a number of Indians in the region in *Aboriginal Relationships between Culture and Plant Life in the Upper Great Lakes Region* [270].

The Siouan-speaking Winnebagos are the only non-Algonquian group in this area. Their material culture, social organization, and religion have been extensively described in Paul Radin's important *The Winnebago Tribe* [150]. Radin also made an extensive study of Winnebago mythology and published a series of books and monographs on the subject. The origin myth of the Medicine Rite, as well as an extended description of the rite itself, is given in his *The Road of Life and Death* [152]. Radin later published the texts themselves in *Winnebago Culture as Described by Themselves* [155]. Winnebago tales are discussed and examples given in *Winnebago Hero Cycles* [153], and the Trickster tales are covered more fully in *The Trickster* [157]. Other myths and stories are given in his *The Evolution of an American Prose Epic* [156] and *The Culture of the Winnebago: As Described by Themselves* [154].

Several Winnebago autobiographies have been published. These include the famous *Crashing Thunder*, edited by Radin [151]; the life of Sam Blowsnake, published by Radin under the title "The Autobiography of a Winnebago Indian" [149]; and *Mountain Wolf Woman, Sister of Crashing Thunder*, edited by Nancy Oestreich Lurie [115].

The history of the Winnebago has been discussed by Publius V. Lawson in "The Winnebago Tribe" [105], and seventeenth-century Winnebago history has been presented more recently by Lurie in "Winne-bago Protohistory" [114].

Of all the Algonquian-speaking peoples in this area, the Menominis are the most extensively described. Felix M. Keesing's ethnohistory of the Menominis, *The Menomini Indians of Wisconsin: A Study of Three Centuries of Cultural Contact and Change* [97], contains not only a history of this group of Indians but also an account of the changes in Menomini culture from about 1634 to 1929. A description of Menomini culture based on fieldwork done at the end of the last century by Walter James Hoffman is published in his *The Menomini Indians* [80] and includes discussions of religious practices, mythology and folktales, social organization, manufactures, and subsistence. The methods used to collect and prepare wild rice are described by Albert Ernest Jenks in *The Wild Rice Gatherers of the Upper Lakes* [86]. As Jenks notes in this comparative study, a number of tribes in the area collected wild rice, but the Menominis were the most dependent on it.

An even more extensive description of Menomini culture than Hoffman's is found in a series of monographs by Alanson Skinner: *Material Culture of the Menomini* [181], *Social Life and Ceremonial Bundles of the Menomini Indians* [178], *Associations and Ceremonies of the Menomini Indians* [179], and (with John V. Satterlee) *Folklore of the Menomini Indians* [180]. Taken together, these four monographs constitute a lengthy ethnography of the Menominis.

The Dream Dance, also called the Drum Religion and the Powwow, introduced about a hundred years ago to the Menominis, has been extensively described by J. S. Slotkin in *The Menomini Powwow* [186], and the more recently introduced peyote religion is covered in Slotkin's *Menomini Peyotism* [185]. A fairly extensive listing of plants used by the Menominis and their uses is given by Huron H. Smith in *Ethnobotany of the Menomini Indians* [188]. A number of Menomini songs and related matters are discussed by Frances Densmore in *Menominee Music* [26].

Various aspects of recent Menomini acculturation are analyzed by George D. Spindler in *Sociocultural and Psychological Processes of Menomini Acculturation* [208] and by Louise S. Spindler in *Menomini Women and Culture Change* [210]. The Spindlers have also written a more popular account of Menomini acculturation, *Dreamers without Power: The Menomini Indians* [209]. It is a very readable account of Menomini reservation life before the reservation was terminated in 1961. An extensive description of the problems faced by the Menominis in the first decade after termination is found in *Freedom with Reservation*, edited by Deborah Shames [171]. It is a case study of the complexities of contemporary Indian affairs, a subject all too infrequently described in print.

Less has been published on the other Algonquian groups in the area than on the Menominis. This is as true for the Sauk and Fox Indians as for the other Algonquian-speakers. The history of these two peoples, whose histories became intertwined in the eighteenth century, is given in William T. Hagan's *The Sac and Fox Indians* [62]. The famous Black Hawk War has been most recently described in Cecil Eby's *"That Disgraceful Affair"* [33], and Black Hawk's autobiography, first published in 1833, is now available in an edition edited by Donald Jackson [8] that contains a useful introduction and notes.

Alanson Skinner has provided a description of Sauk culture in his *Observations on the Ethnology of the Sauk Indians* [182], and William Jones has given a basic description of Fox culture in *Ethnography of the Fox Indians* [96]. The kinship system of the Fox is discussed more fully by Sol Tax in "The Social Organization of the Fox Indians" [219]. Huron H. Smith has provided a description of the plants used by the Fox similar to his description of Menomini plant use in *Ethnobotany of the Meskwaki Indians* [189]. A number of Fox tales, myths, and stories in original text and translation are to be found in William Jones, *Fox Texts* [94]. A Fox woman's account of her own life, also in both original text and translation, is contained in *The Autobiography of a Fox Indian Woman* [119] by Truman Michelson, who published a number of other studies of Fox culture.

In the middle of the nineteenth century, the Fox bought land in Iowa and moved there, where they have remained. This Fox community in the 1930s and the changes in Fox culture as a consequence of contact with Whites have been discussed by Natalie Joffe in "The Fox of Iowa" [89]. A more recent study of this same community by Frederick Gearing, *The Face of the Fox* [54], focuses on the estrangement between the Fox and Whites as a consequence of the differences in their world views.

The history of the Kickapoos is described in A. M. Gibson, *The Kickapoos: Lords of the Middle Border* [55], and in James Silverberg's "The Kickapoo Indians" [176], with special attention to changes in Kickapoo culture from 1640 to 1752. The contemporary life and culture of the Kickapoo Indians who settled in Mexico in the nineteenth century is described briefly by Robert E. Ritzenthaler and Frederick A. Peterson in *The Mexican Kickapoo Indians* [162] and covered more extensively in Felipe A. and Dolores L. Latorre's *The Mexican Kickapoo Indians* [104]. Since this group has preserved to a remarkable degree the culture they had when they lived in the Great Lakes area, these studies contain more useful ethnographic information on older Kickapoo culture than might be supposed. An account of this culture based on information obtained from Kickapoos now living in Oklahoma is found in Ben J. Wallace, "The Oklahoma Kickapoo: An Ethnographic Reconstruction" [245]. Some tales collected by William Jones are published in original text and translation in his *Kickapoo Tales* [95].

Detailed studies have been made of only a few of the now-scattered groups of Potawatomis. Of these, the most extensively described are the Potawatomis who settled on a reservation in Kansas. Ruth Landes has given an account of the kinship and religious practices of this group in *The Prairie Potawatomi: Tradition and Ritual in the Twentieth Century* [103]. These subjects, as well as the folklore and mythology and material culture of this group of Potawatomis were studied earlier by Alanson Skinner, who published the results of his research in *The Mascoutens or Prairie Potawatomi Indians* [183]. The life of the Wisconsin Potawatomis in 1951 has been described by Robert E. Ritzenthaler in *The Potawatomi Indians of Wisconsin* [161], a work that also contains an account of older Potawatomi customs still being practiced. The early history of the Potawatomis is given in Valentine B. Deale, "The History of the Potawatomis before 1722" [24]. Huron H. Smith's *Ethnobotany of the Forest Potawatomi Indians* [190] describes the plants they used.

The most extensive description of Shawnee culture was recorded by C. C. Trowbridge about 1824 and published more than a century later under the title *Shawnese Traditions* [229]. A few studies made in this century have provided additional information on particular aspects of Shawnee culture. These include the following: Erminie Wheeler Voegelin's short account of horticultural practices, "The Place of Agriculture in the Subsistence Economy of the Shawnee" [238]; C. F. and E. W. Voegelin's "Shawnee Name Groups" [234] (these "name groups" of the Shawnees have functions similar to the clans of other North American Indians); C. F. Voegelin's studies of the Creator and her importance in Shawnee religious practice and belief,

*The Shawnee Female Deity* [237] — a role the Voegelin's suggested, in "The Shawnee Female Deity in Historical Perspective" [235] had been a recent development; and Erminie W. Voegelin's "Shawnee Musical Instruments" [239]. The history of the Shawnees is given in Henry Harvey's *History of the Shawnee Indians from the year 1681 to 1854* [69].

Miami and Illinois culture was described by Louis Deliette in his *Memoir concerning the Illinois Country* [136], an account probably written about 1702. (It appears under a title erroneously attributing it to De Gannes.) Another important source of information on these ethnographically poorly known peoples is C. C. Trowbridge's description of Miami culture written in 1825 and published more than a century later under the title *Meearmeear Traditions* [228]. The history of the Miamis from the time of first contact with Whites to the present is given by Bert Anson in his *The Miami Indians* [1]. A brief account of the history of the Illinois is found in Emily J. Blasingham, "The Depopulation of the Illinois Indians" [9].

Among the consequences of White interest in this region was the development of a complex series of tribal alliances and the emergence of Indian leaders whose influence extended to various tribes in times of crisis. The lives of these leaders have been of more than ordinary interest to historians. Recent examples include Howard H. Peckham, *Pontiac and the Indian Uprising* [137], and Glenn Tucker, *Tecumseh: Vision of Glory* [230]. The history of the removal of various Indians of the area — the Sauk and Fox, Potawatomis, Miamis in Indiana, and Ohio Indians — is summarized in Grant Foreman, *The Last Trek of the Indians* [51]. The history of the various Indian groups in Ohio is surveyed in Warren K. Moorehead, "The Indian Tribes of Ohio — Historically Considered" [123] and more extensively in H. C. Shetrone, "The Indian in Ohio" [173].

## ALPHABETICAL LIST AND INDEX

*Denotes items suitable for the general reader.

Item
no.

Essay
page
no.

[1] * Anson, Bert. 1970. *The Miami Indians.*
Norman: University of Oklahoma Press.          (37)

[2] * Barbeau, Charles Marius. 1915. *Huron
and Wyandot Mythology.* Canada: *Geological Survey Memoir* 80. Anthropological
Series II.                                     (23)

[3] * _____. 1960. *Huron-Wyandot Traditional Narratives in Translations and Native
Texts. National Museum of Canada Bulletin*
165 Anthropological Series 47.                 (23)

[4]   Beauchamp, William M. 1907. *Civil,
Religious and Mourning Councils and Cere-
monies of Adoption of the New York Indians.
New York State Museum Bulletin* 113.           (25)

[5] * Biggar, H. P., ed. 1922–36. *The Works of
Samuel de Champlain.* 6 vols. Toronto:
Champlain Society.                             (22)

[6] * _____, ed. 1924. *The Voyages of Jacques
Cartier. Publications of the Public Archives of
Canada* II. Ottawa.                            (22)

[7]   Binford, Lewis R. 1967. "An Ethnohistory of the Nottoway, Meherrin and

Weanock Indians of Southeastern Virginia." *Ethnohistory* 14:103-218.                (20)

[8] * Black Hawk. 1955. *Black Hawk (Ma-ka-tai-me-she-kia-kiak): An Autobiography*, ed. Donald Jackson. Urbana: University of Illinois Press.                (34)

[9]   Blasingham, Emily J. 1956. "The Depopulation of the Illinois Indians." *Ethnohistory* 3:193-224, 361-412.                (37)

[10]   Blau, Harold. 1966. "Function and the False Faces: A Classification of Onondaga Masked Rituals and Themes." *Journal of American Folklore* 79:564-580.    (27)

[11]   Bock, Philip K. 1966. *The Micmac Indians of Restigouche: History and Contemporary Description. National Museum of Canada Bulletin* 213.                (12)

[12]   Boissevain, Ethel. 1956. "The Detribalization of the Narragansett Indians: A Case Study." *Ethnohistory* 3:225-245.    (15)

[13]   _____. 1959. "Narragansett Survival: A Study of Group Persistence through Adopted Traits." *Ethnohistory* 6:347-362.                (15)

[14]   Brasser, Ted J. 1974. *Riding on the Frontier's Crest: Mahican Indian Culture and Culture Change. National Museum of Man*

*Mercury Series Ethnology Division Paper* 13.
Ottawa.                                                    (15)

[15] * Brinton, Daniel G. 1885. *The Lenape and
their Legends.* Philadelphia: D. G. Brin-
ton.                                                       (18)

[16]   Brose, David S. 1973. "The Northeast-
ern United States." In *The Development of
North American Archaeology; Essays in the
History of Regional Traditions,* ed. James E.
Fitting, pp. 84-115. Garden City, N.Y.:
Anchor Books.                                              (10)

[17]   Callender, Charles. 1962. *Social Organi-
zation of the Central Algonkian Indians.
Milwaukee Public Museum Publications in
Anthropology* 7.                                          (30)

[18]   Carse, Mary Rowell. 1949. "The
Mohawk Iroquois." *Bulletin of the Archeological Society of Connecticut* 23:3-53.          (24)

[19] * Chafe, Wallace L. 1961. *Seneca Thanksgiving Rituals. Bureau of American Eth-
nology Bulletin* 183.                                    (26)

[20]   Clarke, Peter Dooyentate. 1870. *Origin
and Traditional History of the Wyandots.*
Toronto: Hunter, Rose.                                   (23)

[21] * Converse, Harriet Maxwell. 1908. *Myths
and Legends of the New York State Iroquois,*
ed. Arthur C. Parker. *New York State
Museum Bulletin* 125.                                    (27)

[22] * Cornplanter, Jesse J. 1938. *Legends of the Longhouse*. Philadelphia: J. B. Lippincott. (27)

[23] * Curtin, Jeremiah, and J. N. B. Hewitt. 1918. "Seneca Fiction, Legends, and Myths." *Bureau of American Ethnology 32nd Annual Report*, 1910–11, pp. 37-813. (27)

[24]   Deale, Valentine B. 1958. "The History of the Potawatomis before 1722." *Ethnohistory* 5:305-360. (36)

[25]   De Forest, John W. 1851. *History of the Indians of Connecticut from the Earliest Known Period to 1850*. Hartford: Wm. J. Hamersley. (Reprinted Hamden, Conn.: Archon Books, 1964.) (16)

[26]   Densmore, Frances. 1932. *Menominee Music. Bureau of American Ethnology Bulletin* 102. (33)

[27] * Denton, Daniel. 1670. *A Brief Description of New York: Formerly Called New Netherlands*. London: John Hancock and William Bradley. (Reprinted, Ann Arbor: University Microfilm.) (16)

[28] * Denys, Nicolas. 1908. *The Description and Natural History of the Coasts of North America (Acadia)*. Trans. and ed. William F. Ganong. Toronto: Champlain Society. (12)

[29] Downes, Randolph C. 1940. *Council Fires on the Upper Ohio: A Narrative of Indian Affairs in the Upper Ohio Valley until 1795.* Pittsburgh: University of Pittsburg Press. (17)

[30] Dragoo, Don W. 1963. *Mounds for the Dead: An Analysis of the Adena Culture. Annals of Carnegie Museum,* Pittsburgh, Pa. vol. 37. (7)

[31] * Driver, Harold E. 1961. *Indians of North America.* Chicago: University of Chicago Press. (5)

[32] Driver, Harold E., and William C. Massey. 1957. *Comparative Studies of North American Indians. Transactions of the American Philosophical Society,* n.s., vol. 47, pt. 2. (5)

[33] * Eby, Cecil. 1973. *"That Disgraceful Affair," The Black Hawk War.* New York: W. W. Norton. (34)

[34] * Eccles, W. J. 1959. *Frontenac: The Courtier Governor.* Toronto: McClelland and Stewart. (8)

[35] * _____. 1964. *Canada under Louis XIV, 1663–1701.* Toronto: McClelland and Stewart. (8)

[36] * _____. 1969. *The Canadian Frontier, 1534–1760*. New York: Holt, Rinehart and Winston.                                    (8)

[37] * _____. 1972. *France in America*. New York: Harper and Row.                                    (8)

[38] Fenton, William N. 1936. *An Outline of Seneca Ceremonies at Coldspring Longhouse. Yale University Publications in Anthropology* 9.                                    (26)

[39] * _____. 1937. "The Seneca Society of Faces." *Scientific Monthly* 44:215-238.                                    (26)

[40] _____. 1940. "Masked Medicine Societies of the Iroquois." *Annual Report of the Smithsonian Institution for 1940*, 397-429.                                    (26)

[41] _____. 1940. "Problems arising from the Historic Northeastern Position of the Iroquois." In *Essays in Historical Anthropology of North America. Smithsonian Institution Miscellaneous Collections* 100:159-251.                                    (21)

[42] _____. 1941. "Tonawanda Longhouse Ceremonies: Ninety Years after Lewis Henry Morgan." *Bureau of American Ethnology Bulletin* 128:139-165.                                    (26)

[43] * _____. 1942. "Contacts between Iroquois Herbalism and Colonial

Medicine." *Annual Report of the Smithsonian Institution for 1941*, 503-526.     (29)

[44]  ———. 1950. *The Roll Call of the Iroquois Chiefs: A Study of the Mnemonic Cane from the Six Nations Reserve. Smithsonian Miscellaneous Collections* 3. no. 15.     (25)

[45]  ———. 1953. *The Iroquois Eagle Dance, An Offshoot of the Calumet Dance. Bureau of American Ethnology Bulletin* 156.     (27)

[46]  Fenton, William N., L. H. Butterfield and Wilcomb E. Washburn. 1957. *American Indian and White Relations to 1830: Needs and Opportunities for Study.* Chapel Hill: University of North Carolina Press.     (4)

[47]  Fenton, William N., ed. 1968. *Parker on the Iroquois.* Syracuse: Syracuse University Press.     (25)

[48] * Fenton, William N. 1971. "The New York State Wampum Collection: The Case for the Integrity of Cultural Treasures." *Proceedings of the American Philosophical Society* 115:437-461.     (29)

[49] * Fitting, James E. 1970. *The Archaeology of Michigan: A Guide to the Prehistory of the Great Lakes Region.* Garden City, N.Y.: Natural History Press.     (6)

[50]    Flannery, Regina. 1939. *An Analysis of Coastal Algonquian Culture. Catholic University of America Anthropological Series* 7.    (11)

[51] * Foreman, Grant. 1946. *The Last Trek of the Indians.* Chicago: University of Chicago Press.    (38)

[52]    Foster, Michael K. 1974. *From the Earth to Beyond the Sky: An Ethnographic Approach to Four Longhouse Iroquois Speech Events. Canadian Ethnology Service Paper* 20, National Museums of Canada.    (26)

[53]    Gallatin, Albert. 1836. *A Synopsis of the Indian Tribes within the United States East of the Rocky Mountains, and in the British and Russian Possessions in North America. Archaeologia Americana, Transactions and Collections of the American Antiquarian Society* 2. (Reprinted New York: AMS Press.)    (5)

[54] * Gearing, Frederick O. 1970. *The Face of the Fox.* Chicago: Aldine.    (35)

[55] * Gibson, Arrell M. 1963. *The Kickapoos: Lords of the Middle Border.* Norman: University of Oklahoma Press.    (35)

[56]    Gookin, Daniel. 1792. "Historical Collections of the Indians in New England." *Massachusetts Historical Society Collections,* 1st series 1:141-227.    (15)

[57]  ———. 1836. "An Historical Account of the Doings and Sufferings of the Christian Indians of New England, in the Years 1675, 1676, 1677." *Archaeologia Americana, Transactions and Collections of the American Antiquarian Society* 2:423-534.                                                    (15)

[58] * Graymont, Barbara. 1972. *The Iroquois in the American Revolution.* Syracuse: Syracuse University Press.          (28)

[59] * ———, ed. 1973. *Fighting Tuscarora: The Autobiography of Chief Clinton Rickard.* Syracuse: Syracuse University Press.     (29)

[60]  Griffin, James B., ed. 1952. *Archeology of Eastern United States.* Chicago: University of Chicago Press.                          (6)

[61]  Guthe, Alfred K., and Patricia B. Kelly. 1963. *An Anthropological Bibliography of the Eastern Seaboard,* volume II. *Eastern States Archeological Federation Research Publication* 2. Trenton, N.J.          (4)

[62] * Hagan, William T. 1958. *The Sac and Fox Indians.* Norman: University of Oklahoma Press.                          (34)

[63]  Hale, Horatio, ed. 1883. *The Iroquois Book of Rites.* Philadelphia: D. G. Brinton. (Reprinted with intro. by William N.

Fenton, Toronto: University of Toronto
Press, 1963.) (25)

[64]  Hallowell, A. Irving. 1960. "The Begin-
nings of Anthropology in America." In
*Selected Papers from the American An-
thropologist, 1888–1920,* ed. Frederica de
Laguna, pp. 1-90. Evanston and New
York: Row, Peterson. (10)

[65]  Harrington, M. R. 1908. "Some Seneca
Corn-foods and their Preparation."
*American Anthropologist* 15:208-235. (28)

[66]  ———. 1913. "A Preliminary Sketch of
Lenape Culture." *American Anthropologist* 15:208-235. (17)

[67] *  ———. 1921. *Religion and Ceremonies of
the Lenape. Indian Notes and Monographs*
19. New York: Museum of the American
Indian, Heye Foundation. (17)

[68] *  Harriot, Thomas. 1588. *A Briefe and
True Report of the New Found Land of Virginia.* London. (Reprinted many times.) (19)

[69]  Harvey, Henry. 1855. *History of the
Shawnee Indians, from the Year 1681 to
1854 Inclusive.* Cincinnati: Ephraim
Morgan and Sons. (Reprinted New
York: Kraus Reprint.) (37)

[70]  Heckewelder, John. 1819. *An Account of*

*the History, Manners, and Customs, of the Indian Nations who once Inhabited Pennsylvania and the Neighbouring States. Transactions of the Historical and Literary Committee of the American Philosophical Society* 1:1-348. (Reprinted New York: Arno Press.) (16)

[71] Heidenreich, Conrad. 1973. *Huronia: A History and Geography of the Huron Indians, 1600–1650.* Toronto: McClelland and Stewart. (22)

[72] Hendry, Jean. 1964. "Iroquois Masks and Maskmaking at Onondaga." *Bureau of American Ethnology Bulletin* 191: 349-409. Anthropological Paper 74. (27)

[73] * Henry, Thomas R. 1955. *Wilderness Messiah: The Story of Hiawatha and the Iroquois.* New York: William Sloane. (24)

[74] * Hertzberg, Hazel W. 1966. *The Great Tree and the Longhouse; the Culture of the Iroquois.* New York: Macmillan. (24)

[75] Hewitt, J. N. B. 1903. "Iroquoian Cosmology. First Part." *Bureau of American Ethnology 21st Annual Report 1899-1900,* pp. 127-339. (27)

[76] _____. 1928. "Iroquoian Cosmology. Second Part." *Bureau of American Ethnol-*

*ogy 43rd Annual Report 1925-26,* pp.
449-819.                                        (27)

[77]    ———. 1944. "The Requickening Address of the Iroquois Condolence Council," ed. William N. Fenton. *Journal of the
Washington Academy of Sciences* 34:65-85.    (25)

[78]    Hicks, George L., and David I. Kertzer.
1972. "Making a Middle Way: Problems
of Monhegan Identity." *Southwestern
Journal of Anthropology* 28:1-24.            (15)

[79]  *  Hodge, Frederick Webb. 1907–1910.
*The Handbook of American Indians North of
Mexico.* 2 vols. *Bureau of American Ethnol-
ogy Bulletin* 30.                            (2)

[80]    Hoffman, Walter James. 1896. "The
Menomini Indians." *Bureau of American
Ethnology 14th Annual Report 1892–93*
(part 2), pp. 3-328.                         (32)

[81]  *  Howley, James P. 1915. *The Beothucks or
Red Indians, The Aboriginal Inhabitants of
Newfoundland.* Cambridge: Cambridge
University Press.                            (11)

[82]  *  Hudson, Charles M. 1970. *The Catawba
Nation. University of Georgia Monographs*
18. Athens: University of Georgia Press.     (20)

[83]    Hulbert, A. B., and W. N. Schwarze, eds.
1910. "David Zeisberger's History of the

Northern American Indians." *Ohio State Archaeological and Historical Quarterly Publications* 19:1-189. (16)

[84] Hulton, Paul, and David Beers Quinn. 1964. *The American Drawings of John White, 1577-1590.* 2 vols. London: Trusteees of the British Museum. Chapel Hill: University of North Carolina Press. (19)

[85] * Hunt, George T. 1940. *The Wars of the Iroquois: A Study in Intertribal Trade Relations.* Madison: University of Wisconsin Press. (9)

[86] Jenks, Albert Ernest. 1900. "The Wild Rice Gatherers of the Upper Lakes: A Study in American Primitive Economics." *Bureau of American Ethnology 19th Annual Report 1897-98,* pp. 1013-1137. (32)

[87] Jennings, Francis. 1968. "Glory, Death, and Transfiguration: The Susquehannock Indians in the Seventeenth Century." *Proceedings of the American Philosophical Society* 112:15-53. (23)

[88] * _____. 1975. *The Invasion of America: Indians, Colonialism, and the Cant of Conquest.* Chapel Hill: University of North Carolina Press. (Re-printed New York: W. W. Norton, 1976.) (15)

[89] * Joffe, Natalie. 1940. "The Fox of Iowa."
In *Acculturation in Seven American Indian
Tribes*, ed. Ralph Linton, pp. 259-331.
New York: D. Appleton-Century.          (35)

[90]   Johnson, Elias. 1881. *Legends, Traditions
and Laws, of the Iroquois, or Six Nations, and
History of the Tuscarora Indians*. Lockport,
N.Y.: Union Printing and Publishing Co.    (29)

[91] * Johnson, Frank Roy. 1967–68. *The Tuscaroras.* 2 vols. Murfreesboro, N.C.:
Johnson Publishing.                       (29)

[92]   Johnson, Frederick. 1943. "Notes on
Micmac Shamanism." *Primitive Man*
16:53-80.                                 (13)

[93]   _____. ed. 1946. *Man in Northeastern
North America. Papers of the Robert S. Peabody Foundation for Archaeology* 3.        (5)

[94] * Jones, William. 1907. *Fox Texts. American Ethnological Society Publication* 1.
(Re-printed New York: AMS Press.)         (34)

[95] * _____. 1915. *Kickapoo Tales,* trans.
Truman Michelson. *American Ethnological Society Publication* 9.            (35)

[96]   _____. 1939. *Ethography of the Fox Indians,* ed. Margaret Welpley Fisher.
*Bureau of American Ethnology Bulletin* 125.   (34)

[97]   Keesing, Felix M. 1939. *The Menomini
Indians of Wisconsin: A Study of Three Cen-*

*turies of Cultural Contact and Change.
American Philosophical Society Memoir* 10.    (32)

[98]    Keppler, Joseph. 1941. *Comments on Certain Iroquois Masks. Museum of the American Indian, Heye Foundation, Contributions* 12, no. 4. New York.    (27)

[99]    Kinietz, Vernon, and Erminie W. Voegelin, eds. 1939. *Shawnese Traditions: C. C. Trowbridge's Account. Occasional Contributions from the Museum of Anthropology of the University of Michigan* 9. Ann Arbor: University of Michigan Press.    (36)

[100]  *  Kinietz, W. Vernon. 1940. *The Indians of the Western Great Lakes, 1615–1760. Occasional Contributions from the Museum of Anthropology of the University of Michigan* 10. Ann Arbor: University of Michigan Press.    (30)

[101]    Kurath, Gertrude Prokosch. 1964. *Iroquois Music and Dance: Ceremonial Arts of Two Seneca Longhouses. Bureau of American Ethnology Bulletin* 187.    (26)

[102]    ———. 1968. *Dance and Song Rituals of Six Nations Reserve, Ontario. National Museum of Canada Bulletin* 220.    (26)

[103]  *  Landes, Ruth. 1970. *The Prairie Potawatomi: Tradition and Ritual in the Twentieth Century.* Madison: University of Wisconsin Press.    (36)

[104] * Latorre, Felipe A. and Dolores L. 1976.
       *The Mexican Kickapoo Indians.* Austin:
       University of Texas Press.                    (35)

[105]   Lawson, Publius V. 1907. "The Win-
       nebago Tribe." *Wisconsin Archeologist*
       6:78-162.                                     (31)

[106] * Leach, Douglas E. 1958. *Flintlock and
       Tomahawk: New England in King Philip's
       War.* New York: Macmillan.                    (15)

[107] * _____. 1966. *The Northern Colonial
       Frontier, 1607–1763.* New York: Holt,
       Rinehart and Winston.                          (8)

[108] * Le Clercq, Chrestien. 1910. *New Relation
       of Gaspesia,* trans. and ed. William F. Ga-
       nong. *Publications of the Champlain Society*
       5. Toronto.                                   (12)

[109] * Leland, Charles G. 1884. *The Algonquin
       Legends of New England, or Myths and Folk
       Lore of the Micmac, Passamaquoddy, and
       Penobscot Tribes.* Boston: Houghton,
       Mifflin.                                      (12)

[110]   Lindeström, Peter, 1925. *Geographia
       Americae with an Account of the Delaware
       Indians Based on Surveys and Notes made in
       1654–1656 by Peter Lindestrom,* trans. and
       ed. Amandus Johnson. Philadelphia:
       The Swedish Colonial Society.                 (16)

[111] * Lorant, Stefan. 1965. *The New World: The First Pictures of America.* Rev. ed. New York: Duell, Sloan and Pearce.                    (19)

[112]    Loskiel, George Henry. 1794. *History of the Mission of the United Brethren among the Indians in North America,* trans. Christian Ignatius La Trobe. London: Brethren's Society for the Furtherance of the Gospel.                    (17)

[113]    Lounsbury, Floyd G. 1968. "One Hundred Years of Anthropological Linguistics." In *One Hundred Years of Anthropology,* ed. J. O. Brew, pp. 150-225. Cambridge: Harvard University Press.    (10)

[114]    Lurie, Nancy Oestreich. 1960. "Winnebago Protohistory." In *Culture in History: Essays in Honor of Paul Radin,* ed. Stanley Diamond, pp. 790-808. New York: Columbia University Press.                    (32)

[115] * _____, ed. 1961. *Mountain Wolf Woman, Sister of Crashing Thunder: The Autobiography of a Winnebago Indian.* Ann Arbor: University of Michigan Press.                    (31)

[116] * Lyford, Carrie A. 1945. *Iroquois Crafts. U. S. Indian Service, Indian Handcrafts* 6. Lawrence, Kansas: Haskell Institute.                    (29)

[117] * Mechling, William Hubbs. 1914. *Male-cite Tales. Canada Department of Mines, Geological Survey Memoir* 49 Anthropological Series 4.    (13)

[118] * _____. 1958–59. "The Malecite Indians, with Notes on the Micmacs." *Anthropologica* 7:1-160; 8:161-274.    (13)

[119] * Michelson, Truman, 1919. The Autobiography of a Fox Indian Woman. *Bureau of American Ethnology 40th Annual Report,* 1918–19, pp. 291-349.    (34)

[120]   Mochon, Marion Johnson. 1968. *Stockbridge-Munsee Cultural Adaptations: "Assimilated Indians." Proceedings of the American Philosophical Society* 112:182-219.    (15)

[121]   Mooney, James. 1894. *The Siouan Tribes of the East. Bureau of American Ethnology Bulletin* 22.    (20)

[122]   _____. 1907. "The Powhatan Confederacy, Past and Present." *American Anthropologist* 9:129-152.    (19)

[123] * Moorehead, Warren K. 1899. "The Indian Tribes of Ohio—Historically Considered." *Ohio State Archaeological and Historical Quarterly* 7:1-109.    (38)

[124] * Morgan, Lewis H. 1851. *League of the Ho-de-no-sau-nee or Iroquois.* Rochester:

Sage and Brother. (Reprint editions: ed. Herbert M. Lloyd. 2 vols. New York: Dodd, Mead and Co., 1901, and New Haven: Human Relations Area Files, 1954; facsimile of 1st ed., intro. by Wm. N. Fenton, New York: Corinth Books, 1962.) (24, 29)

[125] * Morton, Thomas. 1637. *New English Canaan, or New Canaan.* Amsterdam: Jacob Frederick Stam. (Reprinted Boston, *Publications of the Prince Society* 14. 1883.) (14)

[126] Murdock, George Peter, and Timothy J. O'Leary. 1975. *Ethnographic Bibliography of North America.* 4th ed. 5 vols. New Haven: Human Relations Area Files Press. (3)

[127] Newcomb, William W., Jr. 1956. *The Culture and Acculturation of the Delaware Indians. University of Michigan Museum of Anthropology Anthropological Papers* 10. (17)

[128] * Norton, Thomas Elliot. 1974. *The Fur Trade in Colonial New York, 1686–1776.* Madison: University of Wisconsin Press. (9)

[129] * Parker, Arthur C. 1909. "Secret Medicine Societies of the Seneca." *American Anthropologist* 11:161-185. (27)

[130] * _____. 1910. *Iroquois Uses of Maize and other Food Plants. New York State Museum Bulletin* 144. (28)

[131] * ———. 1913. *The Code of Handsome Lake, the Seneca Prophet. New York State Museum Bulletin* 163.    (28)

[132] * ———. 1916. *The Constitution of the Five Nations, or the Iroquois Book of the Great Law. New York State Museum Bulletin* 184.    (25)

[133] * ———. 1923. *Seneca Myths and Folk Tales. Buffalo Historical Society Publication* 27.    (27)

[134] * Parkman, Francis. 1851–1892. *Works.* Many editions, Boston: Little Brown and Co.    (8)

[135] * Parsons, Elsie Clews. 1925. "Micmac Folklore." *Journal of American Folklore* 38:55-133.    (13)

[136]   Pease, Theodore, Calvin, and Raymond C. Werner, eds. 1934. "Memoir of De Gannes Concerning the Illinois Country." *The French Foundations, 1680– 1693. Collections of the Illinois State Historical Library* 23:302-96. [Title is a misattribution. Author should be Louis Deliette.]    (37)

[137] * Peckham, Howard H. 1947. *Pontiac and the Indian Uprising.* Princeton: Princetown University Press.    (37)

[138] Pendergast, James F. and Bruce G. Trigger. 1972. *Cartier's Hochelaga and the Dawson Site.* Montreal: McGill-Queen's University Press. (22)

[139] * Penn, William. 1912. "Letter from William Penn to the Committee of the Free Society of Traders, 1683." In *Narratives of Early Pennsylvania, West New Jersey and Delaware, 1630–1707,* ed. Albert Cook Myers. (J. Franklin Jameson, ed., *Original Narratives of Early American History* 13), 13, pp. 217-244.) New York: Charles Scribner's Sons. (16)

[140] * Petrullo, Vincenzo. 1934. *The Diabolic Root: A Study of Peyotism, the New Indian Religion among the Delawares.* Philadelphia: University of Pennsylvania Press. (17)

[141] Pilling, James Constantine. 1888. *Bibliography of the Iroquoian Languages. Bureau of American Ethnology Bulletin* 6. (4)

[142] ———. 1891. *Bibliography of the Algonquian Languages. Bureau of American Ethnology Bulletin* 13. (4)

[143] Powell, John Wesley. 1881. "Wyandot Government: A Short Study of Tribal Society." *Bureau of American Ethnology 1st Annual Report,* 1879–80, pp. 57-69. (23)

[144]    ———. 1891. "Indian Linguistic Families of America North of Mexico." *Bureau of American Ethnology 7th Annual Report,* 1885–86, pp. 7-142.    (5)

[145] * Quain, Buell H. 1961. "The Iroquois." In *Cooperation and Competition among Primitive Peoples,* ed. Margaret Mead, pp. 240-281. Boston: Beacon Press.    (24)

[146] * Quimby, George Irving. 1960. *Indian Life in the Upper Great Lakes, 11,000 B.C. to A.D. 1800.* Chicago: University of Chicago Press.    (6)

[147] * ———. 1966. *Indian Culture and European Trade Goods: The Archaeology of the Historic Period in the Western Great Lakes Region.* Madison: University of Wisconsin Press.    (6)

[148]    Quinn, David Beers, ed. 1955. *The Roanoke Voyages 1584–1590.* 2 vols. London: Hakluyt Society. 2nd series, 104-105.    (19)

[149] * Radin, Paul. 1920. *The Autobiography of a Winnebago Indian. University of California Publications in American Archaeology and Ethnology* 16:381-473.    (31)

[150] * ———. 1923. "The Winnebago Tribe." *Bureau of American Ethnology, 37th Annual Report,* 1915–16, pp. 35-550.    (31)

[151] * _____, ed. 1926. *Crashing Thunder: The Autobiography of an American Indian.* New York and London: D. Appleton. (31)

[152] * _____. 1945. *The Road of Life and Death: A Ritual Drama of the American Indians.* New York: Pantheon Books. (31)

[153] _____. 1948. *Winnebago Hero Cycles: A Study in An Original Literature. Indiana University Publications in Anthropology and Linguistics. Memoir I;* Supplement to *International Journal of American Linguistics* 14, no. 3. (31)

[154] _____. 1949. *The Culture of the Winnebago: As Described by Themselves. Indiana University Publications in Anthropology and Linguistics Memoir* 2; Supplement to *International Journal of American Linguistics* 15, no. 1. (31)

[155] _____. 1950. *Winnebago Culture as Described by Themselves: The Origin Myth of the Medicine Rite; Three Versions The Historical Origins of the Medicine Rite. Indiana University Publications in Anthropology and Linguistics Memoir 3;* Supplement to *International Journal of American Linguistics* 16, no. 1. (31)

[156] _____. 1954–56. "The Evolution of an American Prose Epic." *Bollingen Foun-*

*dation Special Publications* 3:1-99; 5:103-148. Basel: Ethnographical Museum.    (31)

[157]  *  ———. 1956. *The Trickster: A Study in American Indian Mythology.* New York: Philosophical Library.    (31)

[158]  *  Rainey, Froelich G. 1936. "A Compilation of Historical Data Contributing to the Ethnography of Connecticut and Southern New England Indians." *Bulletin of the Archeological Society of Connecticut* 3:1-89.    (14)

[159]  *  Rand, Silas Tertius. 1894. *Legends of the Micmacs.* New York: Longmans, Green, and Co.    (13)

[160]  *  Ritchie, William A. 1969. *The Archaeology of New York State.* Revised ed. Garden City, N.Y.: Natural History Press.    (6)

[161]  *  Ritzenthaler, Robert E. 1953. "The Potawatomi Indians of Wisconsin." *Public Museum of the City of Milwaukee Bulletin* 19:99-174.    (36)

[162]  *  Ritzenhaler, Robert E., and Frederick A. Peterson 1956. *The Mexican Kickapoo Indians. Public Museum of the City of Milwaukee Publications in Anthropology* 2.    (35)

[163]  *  Ritzenthaler, Robert E. 1969. *Iroquois False-face Masks. Milwaukee Public Museum Publications in Primitive Art* 3.    (27)

[164] * Ritzenthaler, Robert E., and Pat. 1970. *The Woodland Indians of the Western Great Lakes.* Garden City, N.Y.: Natural History Press. (30)

[165] Rouse, Irving, and John M. Goggin. 1947. *An Anthropological Bibliography of the Eastern Seaboard. Eastern States Archeological Federation Research Publication* 1. New Haven. (4)

[166] Ruttenber, Edward Manning. 1872. *History of the Indian Tribes of Hudson's River.* Albany: J. Munsell. (Reprinted by Port Washington, N.Y.: Kennikat Press.) (16)

[167] * Sagard, Gabriel. 1939. *The Long Journey to The Country of the Hurons,* ed. George M. Wrong. *Publications of the Champlain Society,* Toronto. (22)

[168] Sapir, Edward. 1929. "Central and North American Languages." In *Encyclopedia Britannica,* 14th ed., vol. 5, pp. 138-141. (Republished in *Selected Writings of Edward Sapir. In Language, Culture, and Personality,* ed. David G. Mandelbaum. pp. 169-178. Berkeley and Los Angeles: University of California Press, 1949. (5)

[169] * Scott, Duncan C., ed. 1912. "Traditional History of the Confederacy of the Six Nations." *Proceedings and Transactions of*

*the Royal Society of Canada* 3rd series, vol.
5, section II, pp. 195-246.                    (25)

[170]    Sebeok, Thomas A., ed. 1976. *Native
Languages of the Americas* vol. 1; *North
America.* New York and London:
Plenum.                                   (6, 10)

[171]  * Shames, Deborah, ed. 1972. *Freedom
with Reservation: The Menominee Struggle
to Save their Land and People.* Madison:
National Committee to Save the Menom-
inee People and Forests.                       (33)

[172]  * Shea, John Gilmary. 1855. *History of the
Catholic Missions among the Indian Tribes of
the United States, 1529–1854.* New York:
E. Dunigan and Brother.                         (9)

[173]  * Shetrone, Henry Clyde. 1918. "The Indian in Ohio." *Ohio State Archaeological
and Historical Quarterly* 27:273-510.          (38)

[174]  * ———. 1930. *The Mound-Builders: A
Reconstruction of the Life of a Prehistoric
American Race, through Exploration and
Interpretation of Their Earth Mounds, and
Their Cultural Remains.* New York: D.
Appleton.                                        (7)

[175]    Shimony, Annemarie Anrod. 1961.
*Conservatism among the Iroquois at the Six
Nations Reserve. Yale University Publi-
cations in Anthropology* 65.               (24, 27)

[176] Silverberg, James. 1957. "The Kickapoo Indians: First One Hundred Years of White Contact in Wisconsin." *Wisconsin Archeologist* 38:61-181. (35)

[177] * Silverberg, Robert. 1968. *Mound Builders of Ancient America: The Archaeology of a Myth.* Greenwich, Conn.: New York Graphic Society. (7)

[178] * Skinner, Alanson. 1913. *Social Life and Ceremonial Bundles of the Menomini Indians. American Museum of Natural History Anthropological Papers* 13, pt. 1. (32)

[179] * Skinner, Alanson. 1915. *Associations and Ceremonies of the Menomini Indian. American Museum of Natural History Anthropological Papers* 13, pt. 2. (32)

[180] * Skinner, Alanson and John V. Satterlee. 1915. *Folklore of the Menomini Indians. American Museum of Natural History Anthropological Papers* 13, pt. 3. (32)

[181] * _____. 1921. *Material Culture of the Menomini. Indian Notes and Monographs* 20. New York: Museum of the American Indian, Heye Foundation. (32)

[182] * _____. 1923-25. *Observations on the Ethnology of the Sauk Indians. Bulletin of the Public Museum of the City of Milwaukee* 5. (34)

[183] * _____. 1924–27. *The Mascoutens or Prairie Potawatomi Indians. Bulletin of the Public Museum of the City of Milwaukee* 6. (Reprinted Westport, Conn.: Greenwood Press.)    (36)

[184] * _____. 1925. "Some Seneca Masks and Their Uses." *Museum of the American Indian, Heye Foundation, Indian Notes* 2:191-207. New York.    (27)

[185] Slotkin, James S. 1952. *Menomini Peyotism: A Study of Individual Variation in a Primary Group with a Homogeneous Culture. American Philosophical Society Transactions*, n.s. 42, pt. 4.    (33)

[186] _____. 1957. *The Menomini Powwow: A Study in Cultural Decay. Public Museum of the City of Milwaukee Publications in Anthropology* 4.    (33)

[187] * Smith, Erminnie A. 1883. "Myths of the Iroquois." *Bureau of American Ethnology 2nd Annual Report*, 1880–81, pp. 47-116.    (27)

[188] * Smith, Huron H. 1923. *Ethnobotany of the Menomini Indians. Public Museum of the City of Milwaukee Bulletin* 4, no. 1.    (33)

[189] * _____. 1928. *Ethnobotany of the Meskwaki Indians. Public Museum of the City of Milwaukee Bulletin* 4, no. 2.    (34)

[190] * ———. 1933. *Ethnobotany of the Forest Potawatomi Indians. Public Museum of the City of Milwaukee Bulletin* 7, no. 1 (36)

[191] Smith, Nicholas N. 1957. "Notes on the Malecite of Woodstock, New Brunswick." *Anthropologica* 5:1-39. (13)

[192] * Snow, Dean. 1976. *The Archaeology of North America.* New York: Viking Press. (6)

[193] Speck, Frank G. 1909. "Notes on the Mohegan and Niantic Indians." In *The Indians of Greater New York and the Lower Hudson,* ed. Clark Wissler. *American Museum of Natural History Anthropological Papers* 3:181-210. (14)

[194] ———. 1915. "The Eastern Algonkian Wabanaki Confederacy." *American Anthropologist* 17:492-508. (12)

[195] ———. 1915. *The Nanticoke Community of Delaware. Museum of the American Indian, Heye Foundation Contributions* 2, no. 4. New York. (18)

[196] ———. 1919. *Penobscot Shamanism. American Anthropological Association Memoir* 6:239-288. (13)

[197] * ———. 1925. *The Rappahannock Indians of Virginia. Museum of the American Indian,*

*Heye Foundation, Indian Notes and Monographs* 5, no. 3. New York.    (20)

[198]    _____. 1927. *The Nanticoke and Conoy Indians with a Review of Linguistic Material from Manuscript and Living Sources. Papers of the Historical Society of Delaware*, n.s. 1. Wilmington.    (18)

[199] *    _____. 1928. Chapters on *the Ethnology of the Powhatan Tribes of Virginia. Museum of the American Indian, Heye Foundation, Indian Notes and Monographs* 1, no. 5. New York.    (19)

[200]    _____. 1928. "Wawenock Myth Texts from Maine." *Bureau of American Ethnology 43rd Annual Report*, 1925–26, pp. 165-197.    (13)

[201] *    _____. 1931. *A Study of the Delaware Indian Big House Ceremony. Publications of the Pennsylvania Historical Commission* 2. Harrisburg.    (17)

[202] *    _____. 1935. "Penobscot Tales and Religious Beliefs." *Journal of American Folklore* 48:1-107.    (13)

[203]    _____. 1937. *Oklahoma Delaware Ceremonies, Feasts and Dances. American Philosophical Society Memoir* 7.    (17)

[204] *    _____. 1940. *Penobscot Man: The Life History of a Forest Tribe in Maine.* Phila-

delphia: University of Pennsylvania Press.                                    (13)

[205] ———. 1942. *The Tutelo Spirit Adoption Ceremony: Reclothing the Living in the Name of the Dead.* Harrisburg: Pennsylvania Historical Commission.                (20)

[206] * ———. 1945. *The Iroquois: A Study in Cultural Evolution. Cranbrook Institute of Science Bulletin* 23.                      (24, 29)

[207] * ———. 1949. *Midwinter Rites of the Cayuga Long House.* Philadelphia: University of Pennsylvania Press.        (26, 27)

[208] Spindler, George D. 1955. *Sociocultural and Psychological Processes in Menomini Acculturation. University of California Publications in Culture and Society* 5.          (33)

[209] * Spindler, George and Louise. 1971. *Dreamers without Power: The Menomini Indians.* New York: Holt, Rinehart and Winston.                           (33)

[210] Spindler, Louis S. 1962. *Menomini Women and Culture Change. American Anthropological Association Memoir* 91.        (33)

[211] * Squier, E. G. 1849. *Aboriginal Monuments of the State of New York. Smithsonian Contributions to Knowledge* 2.        (7)

[212] * Squier, E. G., and E. H. Davis. 1848.

*Ancient Monuments of the Mississippi Valley. Smithsonian Contributions to Knowledge* 1.                                                              (7)

[213]   Stern, Theodore. 1952. "Chickahominy: The Changing Culture of a Virginia Indian Community." *Proceedings of the American Philosophical Society* 96:157-225.   (20)

[214]   Stites, Sara Henry. 1905. *Economics of the Iroquois. Bryn Mawr College Monographs* 1, no. 3.                                                        (24)

[215] * Stone, William L. 1838. *Life of Joseph Brant — Thayendanegea*. 2 vols. New York: Alexander V. Blake. (Reprinted New York: Kraus Reprint.)          (28)

[216] * ———. 1841. *The Life and Times of Red Jacket, or Sa-go-ye-wat-ha*. New York and London: Wiley and Putnam. (Reprinted St. Clair Shores, Michigan: Scholarly Press.)                                            (28)

[217] * Swanton, John R. 1952. *The Indian Tribes of North America. Bureau of American Ethnology Bulletin* 145.                               (3)

[218] * Tantaquidgeon, Gladys. 1942. *A Study of Delaware Indian Medicine Practice and Folk Beliefs*. Harrisburg: Pennsylvania Historical Commission. (Reprinted 1972 in Gladys Tantaquideon, *Folk Medicine of the Delaware and Related Algonkian In-*

dians. *Pennsylvania Historical and Museum Commission Anthropological Series* 3:1-61.)    (17)

[219]    Tax, Sol. 1937. "The Social Organization of the Fox Indians." In *Social Anthropology of North American Tribes,* ed. Fred Eggan, pp. 241-282. Chicago: University of Chicago Press.    (34)

[220]    Thwaites, Reuben Gold, ed. 1896–1901. *The Jesuit Relations and Allied Documents.* 73 vols. Cleveland: Burrows Bros.    (22)

[221] *  Tooker, Elisabeth. 1964. *An Ethnography of the Huron Indians, 1615–1649. Bureau of American Ethnology Bulletin* 190.    (22)

[222]    ———. 1970. *The Iroquois Ceremonial of Midwinter.* Syracuse: Syracuse University Press.    (26)

[223] *  Trelease, Allen W. 1960. *Indian Affairs in Colonial New York: The Seventeenth Century.* Ithaca: Cornell University Press.    (9, 16)

[224]    ———. 1962. "The Iroquois and the Western Fur Trade: A Problem in Interpretation." *Mississippi Valley Historical Review* 49:32-51.    (9)

[225] *  Trigger, Bruce G. 1969. *The Huron: Farmers of the North.* New York: Holt, Rinehart and Winston.    (22)

[226] *  ———. 1976. *The Children of Aataentsic:*

*A History of the Huron People to 1660.* 2 vols. Montreal: McGill-Queen's University Press.                              (9, 22)

[227] * _____., ed. 1978. *The Northeast.* Vol. 15 of the *Handbook of North American Indians,* general ed. William C. Sturtevant. Smithsonian Institution.                              (3)

[228]    Trowbridge, Charles C. 1938. *Meearmeear Traditions,* ed. Vernon Kinietz. *Occasional Contributions from the Museum of Anthropology of the University of Michigan* 7.                              (37)

[229]    _____. 1939. *Shawnese Traditions* ed. Vernon Kinietz and Erminie W. Voegelin. *University of Michigan Museum of Anthropology Occasional Contributions* 9.                              (36)

[230] * Tucker, Glenn. 1956. *Tecumseh: Vision of Glory.* Indianapolis: Bobbs-Merrill.                              (37)

[231] * Underhill, Ruth Murray. 1953. *Red Man's America.* Chicago: University of Chicago Press.                              (5)

[232] * _____. 1965. *Red Man's Religion.* Chicago: University of Chicago Press.                              (5)

[233] * Vaughan, Alden T. 1965. *New England Frontier: Puritans and Indians, 1620–1675.* Boston: Little, Brown.                              (15)

[234]   Voegelin, Charles F. and E. W. Voegelin.
        1935. "Shawnee Name Groups." *American Anthropologist* 37:617-635.          (36)

[235]   _____. 1944. "The Shawnee Female
        Deity in Historical Perspective." *American Anthropologist* 46:370-375.          (37)

[236] * _____. 1966. *Map of North American Indian Languages. American Ethnological Society Revised Publication* 20.          (5)

[237]   Voegelin, Charles F. 1936. *The Shawnee Female Deity. Yale University Publications in Anthropology* 10.          (37)

[238]   Voegelin, Erminie Wheeler. 1940. "The
        Place of Agriculture in the Subsistence
        Economy of the Shawnee." *Papers of the Michigan Academy of Science, Arts and Letters* 26:513-520.          (36)

[239]   _____. 1942. "Shawnee Musical Instruments." *American Anthropologist* 44:463-475.          (37)

[240]   _____. 1944. *Mortuary Customs of the Shawnee and other Eastern Tribes. Indiana Historical Society Prehistory Research Series* 2, no. 4.          (30)

[241]   *Walam Olum, or Red Score: The Migration Legend of the Lenni Lenape or Delaware In-*

*dians; A new translation, interpreted by linguistic, historical, archaeological, ethnological, and physical anthropological studies,* tr. C. F. Voegelin. Indianapolis: Indiana Historical Society, 1954.                                    (18)

[242] * Wallace, Anthony F. C. 1949. *King of the Delawares: Teedyuscung, 1700–1763.* Philadelphia: University of Pennsylvania Press.                                                        (18)

[243]    _____. 1952. *The Modal Personality Structure of the Tuscarora Indians. Bureau of American Ethnology Bulletin* 150.          (29)

[244] * _____. 1970. *The Death and Rebirth of the Seneca.* New York: Alfred A. Knopf.    (28)

[245]    Wallace, Ben J. 1964. "The Oklahoma Kickapoo: An Ethnographic Reconstruction." *Wisconsin Archaeologist,* n.s. 45:1-69.                                              (35)

[246] * Wallace, Paul A. W. 1946. *The White Roots of Peace.* Philadelphia: University of Pennsylvania Press.                         (25)

[247] * _____. 1961. *Indians in Pennsylvania.* Harrisburg: Pennsylvania Historical and Museum Commission.                            (17)

[248]    Wallis, Wilson D. and Ruth S. 1953. "Culture Loss and Culture Change among the Micmac of the Canadian

Maritime Provinces, 1912–1950."
*Kroeber Anthropological Society Papers*
8/9:100-129. (12)

[249] * _____. 1955. *The Micmac Indians of Eastern Canada.* Minneapolis: University of Minnesota Press. (12)

[250] * _____. 1957. *The Malecite Indians of New Brunswick. National Museum of Canada Bulletin* 148. Anthropological Series no. 40. (13)

[251] Wallis, Wilson D. 1959. "Historical Background of the Micmac Indians of Canada." *National Museum of Canada Contributions to Anthropology* 173:42-63. (12)

[252] * Waugh, Frederick W. 1916. *Iroquois Foods and Food Preparation. Canada Department of Mines Geological Survey Memoir* 86. (28)

[253] * Webb, William S., and Raymond S. Baby. 1957. *The Adena People, No. 2.* Columbus: Ohio Historical Society. (7)

[254] * Webb, William S., and Charles E. Snow. 1945. *The Adena People. University of Kentucky Reports in Anthropology and Archaeology* 7. (7)

[255] Weinman, Paul L. 1969. *A Bibliography of the Iroquoian Literature. New York State Museum and Science Service Bulletin* 411. (4)

[256] * Weslager, C. A. 1943. *Delaware's Forgotten Folk: The Story of the Moors and Nanticokes.* Philadelphia: University of Pennsylvania Press.                    (18)

[257] * _____. 1948. *The Nanticoke Indians, A Refugee Tribal Group of Pennsylvania.* Harrisburg: Pennsylvania Historical and Museum Commission.              (18)

[258] * _____. 1972. *The Delaware Indians: A History.* New Brunswick, N.J.: Rutgers University Press.                            (18)

[259] * Willey, Gordon R. 1966. *An Introduction to American Archaeology.* Vol. I: *North and Middle America.* Englewood Cliffs, N.J.: Prentice-Hall.                            (6)

[260]   Willey, Gordon R. and Jeremy A. Sabloff. 1974. *A History of American Archaeology.* San Francisco: W. H. Freeman.    (10)

[261] * Williams, Roger. 1643. *A Key into the Language of America.* London: Gregory Dexter. (Reprinted Providence: The Rhode Island and Providence Plantations Tercentary Committee, 1936.)        (13)

[262] * Williams, Ted C. 1976. *The Reservation.* Syracuse: Syracuse University Press.    (29)

[263] * Willoughby, Charles C. 1905. "Dress and Ornaments of the New England Indians." *American Anthropologist* 7:499-508.    (14)

[264] * _____. 1906. "Houses and Gardens of the New England Indians." *American Anthropologist* 8:115-132. (14)

[265] * _____. 1907. "The Virginia Indians in the Seventeenth Century." *American Anthropologist* 9:57-86. (19)

[266] * _____. 1935. *Antiquities of the New England Indians.* Cambridge: Peabody Museum of American Archaeology and Ethnology, Harvard University. (14)

[267] * Wissler, Clark. 1940. *Indians of the United States.* New York: Doubleday and Co. (5)

[268] * Wood, William. 1643. *New England's Prospect.* London. (Reprinted Boston: *Publications of the Prince Society* 3, 1865; and New York: Burt Franklin.) (14)

[269] * Wright, Gordon K. 1963. *The Neutral Indians: A Source Book. Occasional Papers of the New York State Archeological Association* 4. Rochester. (23)

[270] Yarnell, Richard Asa. 1964. *Aboriginal Relationships Between Culture and Plant Life in the Upper Great Lakes Region. University of Michigan Museum of Anthropology Anthropological Papers* 23. (31)

Zeisberger's History - see Hulbert and Schwarze [83]

*The Newberry Library*

*Center for the History of the American Indian*

*Founding Director:* D'Arcy McNickle

*Director:* Francis Jennings

Established in 1972 by the Newberry Library, in conjunction with the Committee on Institutional Cooperation of eleven midwestern universities, the Center makes the resources of one of America's foremost research libraries in the Humanities available to those interested in improving the quality and effectiveness of teaching American Indian history. The Newberry's collections include some 100,000 volumes on the history of the American Indian and offer specialized resources for studying historical aspects of Indian-White relations and Indian linguistics. The Center also assists Native Americans engaged in writing tribal histories and developing educational materials.

## ADVISORY COMMITTEE

*Chairman: Alfonso Ortiz*

Robert F. Berkhofer
*University of Michigan*

Robert V. Dumont, Jr.
*Native American Educational Services/Antioch College; Fort Peck Reservation*

Raymond D. Fogelson
*University of Chicago*

William T. Hagan
*State University of New York College, Fredonia*

Robert F. Heizer
*University of California Berkeley*

Nancy O. Lurie
*Milwaukee Public Museum*

Cheryl Metoyer
*University of California, Los Angeles*

N. Scott Momaday
*Stanford University*

Father Peter J. Powell
*St. Augustine Indian Center*

Father Paul Prucha, S.J.
*Marquette University*

Faith Smith
*Native American Educational Services/Antioch College; Chicago*

Sol Tax
*University of Chicago*

Robert K. Thomas
*Wayne State University*

Robert M. Utley
*Advisory Council on Historical Preservation; Washington, D.C.*

Antoinette McNickle Vogel

Dave Warren
*Institute of American Indian Arts*

Wilcomb E. Washburn
*Smithsonian Institution*